Uncut: The Inside Story of Culinary School

By

Patrice Johnson

authorHOUSE™

1663 LIBERTY DRIVE, SUITE 200
BLOOMINGTON, INDIANA 47403
(800) 839-8640
WWW.AUTHORHOUSE.COM

First published by AuthorHouse 09/02/04

ISBN: 1-4184-9066-0 (sc)

Library of Congress Control Number: 2004096058

Printed in the United States of America
Bloomington, Indiana

This book is printed on acid-free paper.

Illustrations by Joy Johnson

Book Dedication

To: Randy, my partner, and
Nia, my savior
To my Mom for special memories in Pasadena, and to
my Dad for all of his help.
With special love to my husband, he deserves a medal!
To my dear friend Carol, thanks for your kind moral support and for
encouraging me to follow my dreams.
To the fellow culinary students in my class, YOU made this a reality!
To Chef Steve at Albion River Inn who made my externship the most
positive experience and who taught me the things that I've needed
the most.
To all my friends and to my students in my fitness classes who believed
in me, this book is for you!
With love,

Chef Patrice

Table of Contents

Uncut - Chapter 1
Prologue

The kitchen is spotless. Of all the things that we notice, we notice that first. It is downright sparkling! The student's jackets look white and crisp and fresh. As they open their tool kits with great pride, we notice how they run their fingers carefully over their knives before taking them from their protective sleeves. They are all sporting new notebooks and their pockets hold pens and an instant read thermometer. They look so impressive!

My best friend and I are peering through the windows of a popular cooking school in southern California. We are trying really hard to take it all in. For one thing, the size of the kitchens is unbelievable and the chef instructors look so impressive in their tall chef hats and white coats! We are looking at the expressions of the students who are diligently following the instructor's every word. We make sure to notice the vast amount of equipment, particularly the 20 plus stoves and ovens with pans hanging above each one, dishwashing sinks and all of the stainless steel preparation tables. The equipment fills what seem to be endless steel racks along the sides of the room. There is a whole wall of refrigerators and freezers and there are incredible pots that you wouldn't believe the size of! The students we are watching are running frantically around the kitchen gathering up the things they need for their day of cooking. Incredibly, the chef instructors seem to remain poised and calm in the front of their desks, gazing almost nonchalantly at the students as they look down at their laptop computers.

A list of cooking times is posted on a dry erase board with each students name and the time that their creation is due.

As we look, a passerby stops us and asks us if this is a cooking school. "Yes, we say, it is a cooking school with a Cordon Bleu certification program." "Really?" he quizzes. He looks rather stunned and said that he had no idea this school was even here. He asks us if we attend this school. We nod our heads and laugh. We remember that it wasn't long ago that we didn't know this school was here either, but today we are saying good-bye to the place where we have spent more hours than we can count. Our jackets are worn and gray, our knives scratched, our bodies are down right whipped, and our minds overly burdened. We are no where near the same people we were when we arrived here one year ago. We explain to the curious one that today is our last day at this very culinary school.

As we say good-bye to the stranger we take one more glance at the students in the classroom and we reminisce about what it has taken for us to accomplish this overwhelming task over the past year to become chefs. With emotions running strong on this, our last day, we don't know whether to laugh or to cry.

My friend and I are desperately trying to remember how we felt one year ago when we started school. We looked in that window one more time, to try to see it the way we once did as we toured the school and dreamed of being in that classroom. But today we are hard pressed to remember that innocence and the excitement of what we were about to undertake.

One thing that does stand out in our minds though is the many friends and family members who all said the exact same thing when we told them that we were going to culinary school. "I've always wanted to do that. It sounds like so much fun!" Many days over the past year we have tried to explain to them that culinary school isn't what they think it is going to be, but they don't believe us.

The stranger asks, "So, what was it like? Is it a good school?"

Here is the uncut, real story that will take you inside the walls of culinary school to see what it is really like. Get your knife sharpened and come along!

Patrice Johnson

SHOULD I?

Uncut - Chapter 2
Deciding to go to School

One thing that made my culinary experience particularly challenging was the fact that I lived 2 ½ hours away from the school. When I started school, I considered having to make the commute to be a big advantage. I thought it would be great because during the week I could be near school, and then I could come home every weekend, and my husband and I could enjoy fun romantic picnics during the days, and entertain our friends with elegant gourmet meals in the evenings.

I had been an at home gourmet cook for many years and let's face it, I knew what I was doing. This was simply going to be making it official. A mere formality.

My only work in the food industry was brief. It consisted of a short stint at a local French restaurant where I made crème brulee. I got this job in an odd way. The restaurant was new and my husband and I went there one evening for dinner. Our town has very few fine dining restaurants and so people were waiting in line to get into this one. I was very excited. It seemed to have the ambiance that it should possess and the menu looked fantastic. Although I had never considered any type of culinary career before, I knew on that first evening that I wanted to work there. My husband and I had a few glasses of wine while we waited for our dinner and by the time dessert came we had enjoyed several more glasses of wine. It was just about that time that the owner of the restaurant wandered out to see how everyone was doing. When he came over to our table I told him how impressed I was with the restaurant, but expressed to him that I was very disappointed that they did not serve crème brulee. He told me that he didn't know how to make crème brulee and that maybe I could teach him. I told him I make crème brulee every day. Okay, in reality I had made it a half dozen times, but I figured that qualified me as an expert. He told me he might give me a call and I laughed, sipping my wine.

The next day at eleven in the morning, the phone rang. It was the restaurant owner! He wanted to know if I could come to the restaurant and make him some crème brulee. "Of course," I said nonchalantly, and asked him "What time?" He said "How about in a half hour?" I hung up the phone and ran to tell my husband. I explained that there was no way I could go down there and make crème brulee without a recipe. I was going to look like an idiot. "How could I make it with someone watching me?" I asked my husband, and even more importantly, how would I caramelize the top?? You see, up until that day I had never operated a blowtorch. My husband had always finished the brulee for me, and now I had a half hour to get comfortable with caramelizing that sugar on the top. In my opinion it isn't a good crème brulee if you can't tap your spoon against the rock hard sugar coating. And since on this particular day I didn't have any crème brulee baked to practice with, I was going to have to wing it.

I guess it must have been a life changing moment for me on that day. In fact, I know now that it most definitely was! When I got hired to work in that restaurant, I already held a full time job in a field completely unrelated to restaurant work. I had never worked in a restaurant in my life, but now I was spending every spare weekend moment baking there. I know it was then that I fell in love with being in a professional kitchen. After several months I found myself rearranging my other job schedule so that I could spend more and more time at the restaurant. I didn't know it then, but those crème brulees changed my life forever. While I had never done more than tinker in the restaurant business, cooking had been a big hobby for me for several years. Now, things were different. I wanted to really know what I was doing. I wanted the schooling that would make me a professional.

There were lots of months spent looking into culinary schools, arranging tours of the schools, and pouring over culinary school brochures, but most of all figuring out if I could really afford to quit my full time job AND pay for the cost of culinary school.

In my mind, this formal schooling was pretty much just to formalize what I already knew and to learn some neat tricks of the trade. I really wanted to learn how to hold a pastry bag correctly, and also learn how to make cream puffs and éclairs, since those were skills that I had not been able to master at home. Other than that, I figured culinary school would be a breeze. Therefore, it was an easy decision for me to quit my full time job at a local fitness center.

I guess I have to admit that it seemed very exciting to be going back to school again. Everyone I talked to said that they had always wanted to go to culinary school. They asked me if I aspired to Emeril, The Naked Chef, or Mario, and I had no idea to whom they were referring. You see, I had never even seen the Food TV Network!

The way that I felt the week prior to school was an amazing high of excitement. I loved my new chef outfit and my brand new tool kit and all my books. I just couldn't wait to get started and to become a real chef! I remember very nonchalantly telling my husband that this was going to be a life-changing event for me. But trust me, I had no idea to what extent!

The school was on a brand new campus. I was given a wonderful tour of the campus where they showed me those beautiful new kitchens worth hundreds of thousands of dollars, and I was impressed immediately. If you wanted to be in a professional kitchen, then there can be no doubt this was the place to be!

The school featured a fine dining restaurant, café, retail store, Consumer Education Center and an extensive culinary library. It housed 18 teaching labs and 9 classrooms.

I selected the school because they possess the prestigious reputation of Le Cordon Bleu. This certification is considered to be the gold standard in the cooking industry.

It represents an internationally renowned school for the culinary arts and has become synonymous with expertise, innovation, tradition and refinement; qualities which are painstakingly nurtured by the school. Founded in Paris in 1895, Le Cordon Bleu's name traces back to a high honor bestowed upon members of the Holy Spirit by King Henry III in the 1500's. The awarded medallion, called the Cross of the Holy Spirit, was suspended from a Blue Ribbon or Le Cordon Bleu.

This school is only one of a handful of cooking schools in the United States that is in partnership with the legendary French cooking institute to offer this highly regarded curriculum. That was all I needed to know to sign on the dotted line. And that is about all I really did know about Cordon Bleu. It was the best, so I should attend it. That made sense to me.

VANILLA BEAN CRÈME BRULEE
Serves 4

2 cups whipping cream
½ cup granulated sugar
3 large egg yolks
½ vanilla bean

Cut vanilla bean open and scrape seeds into medium saucepan.
Add whipping cream.
Scald whipping cream, but do not boil.
Whisk egg yolks and sugar together.
Gradually introduce a portion of the hot mixture into the egg yolk mixture.
Whisk quickly so that you do not cook the eggs.
Strain mixture. This is important to make your crème brulee very silky.
Pour mixture into four custard cups or crème brulee dishes if you have them.
Place dishes on a baking sheet with a lip.
Fill baking sheet with water so that it comes up halfway on the sides of the custard cups.

Bake in 300 degree oven until just set. You want to see the center of
the custard looking slightly underdone when you take them out of
the oven. They will continue to set up in the refrigerator.

Cool and then cover and refrigerate for at least 4-6 hours.

I usually make mine the day before I need them.

Just before serving, sprinkle one teaspoon of granulated sugar on the
top of each custard. Shake the custard dish gently against your
counter to evenly distribute the sugar.

Using a blow torch, melt the sugar as quickly as you can.

Be careful not to take too long or to stay in one place for a long time or
you will begin to cook the custard.

You may refrigerate for 5-10 minutes after the brulee is done, or serve
immediately.

VANILLA ORANGE CRÈME BRULEE
Serves 2

3 egg yolks
2 tablespoons sugar
One cup heavy whipping cream
Orange zest (1 tablespoon)
½ vanilla bean

Whisk egg yolks and sugar.
Scald cream with orange zest and vanilla.
Temper into egg mixture.
Stir to combine and thicken slightly.
Remove from heat.
Strain.
Pour into ramekins.
Bake at 300 degrees on sheet tray in a water bath as described above.
Chill.

Just before serving sprinkle one teaspoon of granulated sugar on the
top of each custard. Shake the custard dish gently against your
counter to evenly distribute the sugar.

Patrice Johnson

Uncut - Chapter 3
The First Day of School

School began on a Monday and I was absolutely excited in every way. First of all I had on my beautiful, crisp, new chef's jacket and I thought the checkered hounds tooth pants even looked pretty awesome. I had no idea how to wear the neckerchief, so I packed that in my book bag along with my apron and floppy white hat. I gathered up my tool kit, actually a bit gingerly. The week before while showing a friend my knives, I had immediately been grazed by one and I realized that they are as sharp as scalpels. I'm not touching those knives again until an instructor is near by. That much I know for sure.

I am very anxious to see what we are going to be cooking today. Sure, I know we are going to have a little history and sanitation to discuss, but the big deal is the cooking! I decide that whatever I make today is going to be absolutely wonderful. I am already imagining that whatever I learn I will take home with me this weekend and practice. I want the experience to be perfect, and in my mind I am just absolutely convinced that it will be nothing less than that.

11

Patrice Johnson

When I arrived at the school I saw a sign on the door "Welcome New Students". I felt so special! I quickly walked to the kitchen lab for my class and walked in. The first thing that I noticed was that there were many more people in that room than I had been expecting. By the time the class began there were 36 students sitting there. I got a bit nervous and started counting stoves. Was there really going to be room for all of us in this kitchen? I was imagining the workspace I have in my own kitchen at home and with the price of this school, I couldn't imagine that I should have anything less. I figured that any moment someone would be coming in to split up this large group and we would have the 15 students per class as promised. It was not to be. It seemed that there were two classes starting today, each with 36 students. In addition, we were told to put our hats and knife kits away. We wouldn't be needing them for two weeks. Two weeks??? But how can you cook without your knife kit I thought.

We quickly learned that our entire day would consist of academics only for the first two weeks. What was I going to tell my friends? What was I going to cook for them this weekend to show off my newfound skills?

Just when we thought it couldn't get any better, a chef instructor walked into the room. He said good morning to everyone and not getting the response he expected, actually began to snarl at us. He walked around the room snarling at some people individually and even pulling some aside to point out that they didn't have the right kind of shoes on. It was just then as I sank low into my seat, that a very cheerful chef came into the room and greeted us all. He smiled and welcomed us and seemed to be the complete opposite of the other chef instructor. After a while it became apparent to me that one of these instructors would be my Intro I instructor and I prayed with everything I had in me that it would not be the snarler.

As the week went on I continued to get emails and phone calls from friends and family, and everyone wants to know "what's cooking?" How could I explain to my friends and family that this entire week has been spent in the classroom learning about the history of food in the morning, and sanitation in the afternoon. The classes are held in the large kitchen laboratories of the school with their twenty-some ovens, stoves, and hundreds of hanging utensils. Having to attend class in the kitchen seems to add insult to injury. Everyone is antsy and it is hard to pay attention to long lectures about the history of food. Now, c'mon I'm thinking, I had enough history in college. I'm ready to get cracking here. I want to learn how to use those doggone knives because they really scare me to death. The last thing I need to know is food history.

We learned that the premise of what our school was teaching us was the basics behind the food industry. We were also in for a full day of first aid training. This is making my stomach queasy and the knives are no closer to coming out of their case than they were a week ago.

The sanitation lectures have been a wealth of information. Food safety is non-negotiable. Serving safe food is of the utmost importance. We learn that it is our obligation as food service professionals. The most important things that we have learned are how to prevent food borne illnesses (food poisoning). Being cleanly is definitely #1. Food exposed to the time-temperature danger zone (between 41 and 140 degrees) for more than four hours is at the highest risk. Therefore, it is extremely important to keep hot foods HOT (above 140 degrees) and cold foods COLD (less than 41 degrees). Hand washing is critical. Our instructor told us that if you work in a kitchen, you can't wash your hands often enough.

In history we learned that in pre-historic times, people basically ate whatever they could find. Now folks, let's face it, we're way beyond that by now. Can we please just get cooking?

If it isn't bad enough that we haven't sniffed a morsel of food yet in these kitchens, let's talk about homework! Yep, every night we have lots of reading to do and long lists of terms to define. All the free time I had been looking forward to seems to be eaten up every night in front of the computer. Oh, this is lots of fun I think imagining everyone who told me that they always wanted to attend culinary school.

At the end of week one we all took the ServSafe program (sanitation) exam. A passing grade means that I will receive a ServSafe certificate from the National Restaurant Association. I think it also means that I can continue in culinary school. I also took the Food History "mid-term." Passing that will result in no certificate, just the self-satisfaction that I have survived the course so far.

Patrice Johnson

GRILLED MARINATED CHICKEN

1 cup soy sauce
¾ cup extra virgin olive oil
¾ cup red wine vinegar or red wine
1 tablespoon oregano leaves
Two tablespoons basil leaves
One tablespoon garlic powder
One teaspoon black pepper, freshly ground (or to taste)

Mix all ingredients together with a whisk.
Place chicken pieces in marinade in large plastic bag and let set
    overnight in refrigerator.
Grill chicken on a very hot, well-oiled grill.

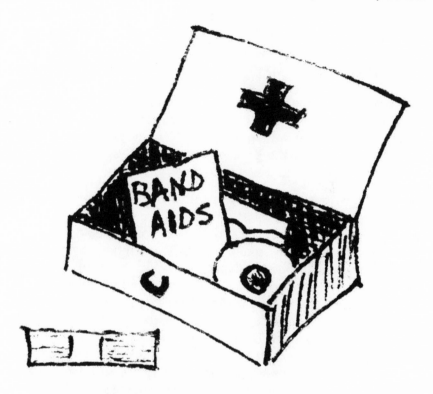

Uncut - Chapter 4
Chemistry, First Aid and Slice

Week two of culinary school is over and we are now finished with food history, and of all things, food science & chemistry! We have received our next class assignment, Introduction to Culinary I, which is where I will spend the next four weeks. In this class we will begin hands-on work including classic knife cuts, terminology, equipment of the kitchen, measurements, stocks, soups and basic pasta dishes.

I don't know about you, but I remember my high school chemistry classes with horror! I had no idea how much chemistry would be involved in cooking, but I was finding out that there is quite a bit more than I bargained for!

What in the world are we doing with chemistry? Was that really the periodic table that the instructor flashed up on the overhead projector?

Turns out chemistry is a big part of cooking! All foods contain some water (hydrogen). Some foods, like eggs, milk and leafy vegetables are composed almost entirely of water. As the internal temperature of food increases, water molecules move faster and faster until the water turns to a gas, which we know as steam and then it vaporizes. This evaporation of water is responsible for the drying of foods during cooking. We spent much of our time learning about coagulation, which deals with how proteins cook. Once a protein coagulates, it hardens and is irreversible. For example, think of the protein in egg whites. Once you scramble eggs, it is not possible to unscramble them! Who knew?

Our hands on science experiments included making butter and cheese. We also saw how yeast grows. To make your own fresh butter at home, fill a large canning jar with two cups of whipping cream. Turn off the TV and take turns among your family members shaking the jar until the cream pulls together (what is known in chemistry as breaking up the phospholipid membranes which are the fat globules in cream.) As you churn (shake) the cream liquid, these globules are emulsified. When you are finished making your butter, there will be a solid mass as well as liquid in your jar. Drain off the liquid which is buttermilk, and you will be left with fresh butter. This process took us about 30 minutes in class, although we may have been shaking the jar a bit zealously! And don't forget there are 36 shakers. Amazingly, the second jar in class never turned to butter. Now here is a little clue that I learned early on in culinary school. The teachers really enjoy having fun at our expense. This time our teacher had tricked us by putting non-dairy creamer in the jar! Only real cream can be used to make butter. Add zest to your homemade butter by adding fresh garlic and herbs. Won't your dinner guests be impressed when you serve homemade butter? Remember that your butter will be a bit lighter in color than that you purchase in the store. Since it won't have preservatives, you will want to use it within a week.

It's week three at culinary school and the moment we've all been waiting for is about to begin. We are going to get the knife kits out and start cooking!

We finished last week with a half-day of first aid. The course was very specific to the "hostile kitchen environment." which is where we find ourselves this week. Once we broke out our knife sets it didn't take long for the bloodletting to begin. In fact, I had not yet removed the protective sleeve from my knife when the first cut occurred. The victim was quickly nicknamed 'Slice', a name which he carried with him throughout our days in culinary school. I was really upset that someone actually got cut. In those days I was very naïve regarding how dangerous the kitchen environment really is. When I expressed my concern to the chef instructor, he assured me that getting cut is really quite common. He is so nonchalant and I am shocked that he simply refers to these incidences as "first-aid situations."

What's interesting is that nobody paid much attention to Slice as he sat at the front of the classroom with his arm elevated above his shoulder while the teacher applied pressure to his brachial artery. This, in order to stop the bleeding. Yes, I remember that we did learn about that in the first aid class. Slice was very embarrassed and was seriously contemplating dropping out of culinary school. He wouldn't have been the first. In two weeks, we had already lost three students. After elevating his arm for 20 minutes, the chef instructor decided that Slice was going to be okay. Okay defined that he wasn't going to have to go to the emergency room. In a few minutes he was back at his cutting board gingerly holding his knife. I couldn't seem to take my eyes off of him and this made me even more scared to pick up the large chefs knife in front of me. However, the chef instructor assured me that you will only get cut if you are afraid. I told him I was petrified which I figured guaranteed me a trip to the emergency room. I think he thought I was kidding, but I was actually frightened to pick up that chef knife. I was used to cutting everything at home with small steak knives. Knife skills were definitely something I needed to pick up at culinary school since they were not in my area of expertise.

The instructors have not yet taught us how to sharpen our knives because, as I'm sure you are surmising, they are already very sharp. We learned today though, that factory-edged knives are not at their sharpest and should be sharpened when first used.

My instructor gave me some one-on-one tips (no pun intended) and, as a result, I feel much more comfortable with my knives. I am happy to report that I made it the entire week without being one of the "first-aid situations". There were three total first aid situations that week. Two of which required stitching at the local hospital. One of the students was rather shaken up. He told me that the school called a cab for him and he had to ride by himself to the hospital. Not only that, he had to pay for the cab when he got there! Several weeks later he was still nursing an ugly wound from that first week with the knives. Beyond the bloodletting, most of the rest of the week was spent learning to make soup stocks.

If you are considering attending culinary school, you may be interested in knowing what the day consists of. Mine begins at 5 a.m. Usually I am finishing up some of the previous evening's homework that I failed to complete in the three hour window the chef instructor stated it would take. At that time, I am also ironing and starching my uniform. This is commonly known as multitasking. Chefs are expert multi-taskers! Our chef's uniform consists of a stiff, cotton white jacket and hound's tooth (black & white) pants. Our jacket is embroidered with the Le Cordon Bleu emblem and blue ribbon on one side, and our name on the other side. We have a starched white apron, two white side towels and our toque (pronounced tōk), which is French for chef's hat. Our hat is not the tall toques you are used to seeing. It is a floppy toque and looks rather silly. On the first day of class the instructor shows us how to wear the toque. He tells us that he doesn't want to see other variations of the toque. Basically the toque is put on and closed with a piece of Velcro. When I place mine on, it usually flops to one side. I can't conceive of any other way to wear it, but you would absolutely not believe the number of variations that I saw during my year at school. People stood the hat up straight so it looked more like the chef instructors hat. They wrapped the Velcro around the material a few times and made the hat look small and tight. A few students always made the hat look as though it had a large plate inside the top of it. The toque it seems was the only way we could personalize our outfit.

Class begins promptly at 8:00 a.m. and we take no breaks. Our day ends when the kitchen has been cleaned up to the satisfaction of our chef instructors; ideally at 2:30, but typically around 3:00 p.m. It always seemed to be later on Fridays. Each evening comprises a three hour session of homework including reading, writing essays, vocabulary, and studying for quizzes and tests. Oh, make sure you set aside some time to hone your knife skills.

Speaking of clean up, let me explain how this works. Each week we are assigned a different task. These fun chores range from dishes to stove clean up with everything else in between. It is the end of our very first week of cooking and I'm on dish duty. Dish sinks are comprised of a triple sink. The first has hot soapy water, the second, hot plain water and the last sink is a rinse station. No dishes actually get dried in the professional kitchen, because this is considered unsanitary! We are nearly finished with all of our dishes when Lonnie, one of the students, comes over to wash his knives. Now, folks, just so you get the picture here, I want to make sure you understand that Lonnie has THE most expensive knives. He could not have the ones that came with our knife kit, but instead purchased a top of the line very sleek and lightweight set of knives. Since we are all still getting used to seeing these elegant knives, I watched him carefully as he brought one over to the dish sink to clean it. As he ran it under the soapy water, I watched in shock as he lifted it up and ran his other hand right down the edge of the knife. Instantly the water turned red. He had cut his hand, and pretty badly at that. I quickly yelled for the chef instructor who came running. Next, Lonnie left for the hospital. I think all of us were a little less impressed with those fancy knives after that afternoon.

Patrice Johnson

Uncut - Chapter 5
We're Really Cooking At Last!

I learned how to make stocks this week. What you will learn in culinary school that you didn't know as an at home gourmet cook, is that stocks are considered to be the foundation of all really good soups and sauces. If you were like me, anytime a recipe called for a stock you just substituted a bouillon cube. Same thing, right? Wrong! Stocks are one of the most important basics that a chef must know how to make. Once you taste soups and sauces made with stocks you will know that you truly can never go back to your bouillon cubes. The next weekend at home, I promptly threw mine away. They were beneath me now! I was boiling a huge pot of veal bones on the stove and my husband was just shaking his head and muttering that this was absolutely incredible.

After the stock making we all went out to buy veal bones. They are not easy to find and we didn't really know what to ask for when we did find them. My friend ordered some bones from a local butcher and took them home. She took a look around her small apartment and at her stockpot and realized that the huge bones would never fit. They were veal leg bones, which had not been cut. She did her best to cut them smaller using her knife kit. By the time she had browned the bones in the oven, the fire alarm was going off in her apartment building and neighbors were running towards her door to see what was going on. She assured them not to worry, because she was in fact a culinary student and she knew what she was doing! I was sure to ask the butcher to chop my veal bones small.

In addition to the crises at home, crises are now beginning to occur on a regular basis at school. We are now running frantically around the kitchen and trying to make food, find the proper pots, pans, and tools to get everything done within the time limits imposed by our chef instructors. I'm thinking that I don't remember the time issue being discussed on my tour of the school. I've never done this stuff before, I'm still learning, this is a school, right? Why are we being timed?

Here's how it works. The chef instructors, demonstrate everything that we will make for the day. Watching them is extremely entertaining and they make everything look fun and easy. When my partner and I get over to the stoves and try to replicate what they've shown us, we feel like we're not even preparing the same dish! But it looked so easy when they did it! Of course, as our chef instructors remind us, they have years of experience. Forget the experience you think you have as an at home cook. In these professional kitchens under the ever-watchful eyes of the chef instructors, everything changes.

One of the neatest things that we are learning is how to cook without a recipe. We learn ratios for everything, which means I can make one gallon of soup, or I can make 10 gallons without a recipe. Wow! What am I going to do with that huge buffet cabinet at home full of recipes? Will I now know how to cook everything without a recipe? Not cooking with a recipe seemed very foreign to me, but this weekend, as I made homemade macaroni and cheese from a Béchamel sauce, I realized that it is really easy! Of course we are talking about macaroni and cheese, not exactly a gourmet delight, but it is a start. It is amazing, for those of us who think we know something about cooking, to go to school and feel totally awkward in the kitchen. Alas, we quickly find out we've been doing most of it wrong.

Almost everyone enjoys a great French Onion Soup, however I've never tasted one as fantastic as the one we made in class. Now you can make it too! Just give yourself a few days notice to make your veal stock. You are well ahead of the game, since you know how to get your veal bones cut. This recipe is time consuming, but worth the effort. Now, let's cook Cordon Bleu style! The secret of really great French Onion Soup is to start with a rich brown stock. To make one you will need the following:

BROWN VEAL STOCK

5-6 lbs. veal bones
1 lb. vegetables (mirepoix) 50% onions, 25% carrots, 25% celery
    chopped uniformly in size
½ cup white wine or water
½ cup tomato products (see below)
herbs (bay leaf, a few whole peppercorns, and a sprig of thyme)
5 – 6 quarts water
8 oz. Madeira wine

Brown stocks can be differentiated from white stocks by the fact that
    the bones and the mirepoix are browned for the stock. Brown
    stocks are made by browning bones, vegetables and other
    ingredients before adding them to the liquid. Bones are roasted
    in a moderately heated oven until they are well browned. Make
    sure they achieve a dark caramel brown color. Occasionally stir the
    bones to make sure that they are browning in an even manner.
    Once the bones have been browned, drain the fat from the bones
    and place them in a stockpot filled with cold water. Note: While
    browning the bones it is usually a good idea to turn off all smoke
    detectors. Cold water is a secret to making stocks. Heat the water
    to a simmer. Make sure you have enough water to cover the bones
    completely. Do not boil. Boiling stocks will make them cloudy and
    this you definitely do not want to achieve.
Instead of the oven, place the pan on the top of stove. Add your
    vegetables (mirepoix) to the pan and brown them. Add the
    browned mirepoix to the stockpot.
Now it is time to deglaze your pan. You're in culinary school now, so
    impress your friends with the professional cooking terms! Take a
    spoon and scrape the pieces of fat and bones stuck to the bottom
    of your pan to loosen them and then add the wine. Add the liquid
    from this pan to the stockpot.
After the vegetables have been browned evenly, add tomato products
    (canned tomatoes, fresh tomatoes, tomato puree, tomato paste,
    your choice) to the stockpot and continue to simmer. The object is
    to remove the raw taste of the tomatoes. Be careful not to burn the
    mixture since tomato products tend to burn quickly.
The stock should simmer a minimum of 6-8 hours (and up to 48 hours!)
    I usually do mine overnight. Add the Madeira wine near the end of
    your cooking time so that the entire flavor does not cook out. As

your stock cooks, you will want to skim it frequently to remove fat and scum. Finally, you should strain your stock and cool it.

In school we used large ice popsicles (about 3 feet long) to stir the stock and help it cool faster. You can simulate this at home by freezing a large water bottle.

After your stock is cooled to 70 degrees you should refrigerate it. Stock may also be frozen and taken out of the freezer, as you need it to make soups. You will need this stock to make your French Onion Soup.

FRENCH ONION SOUP

In a large pot, sauté one pound of sliced sweet onions in approximately one half stick of unsalted butter, over a low heat until they are heavily caramelized. This brings out the sweetness in the onions. Carmelization must be done at a low-medium heat or the onions will burn. Use Vidalia onions if you can get them since they are extra sweet.

Add 2 cups veal stock, 2 cups water, ¼ cup dry white wine, salt and pepper to taste.

Top soup with a crouton and cheese.

Croutons for French onion soup:

Slice day old French bread into thin slices. Brush bread slices with melted butter or dunk the bread in melted butter. Sprinkle pepper on the bread. Toast on cookie sheet. For each crouton, grate Gruyére cheese on top and melt in the oven or under a broiler. Gruyére cheese has a 55% fat content so it melts fast. Substitute Swiss cheese only if you cannot get Gruyére.

Uncut - Chapter 6
All About Eggs

This week was all about eggs! We learned to make them just about every way imaginable. The instructor informed us that he had 350 eggs for us to cook today! I'm going to share some tips with you that will make your eggs the best they have ever been.

The most important point we learned, was to cook eggs with clarified butter. Let me explain why. Clarified butter has a higher smoke point than regular butter, which means it can be used to cook with at hotter temperatures, such as sautéing. It doesn't burn as easily as regular butter. If you use it to cook your eggs, you will have gleaming white eggs, not greasy brown ones. Make sure that you cook eggs at a low temperature.

Butter that has been clarified is also known as drawn butter. Frequently you will see drawn butter served with lobster and I'm sure you can recall how clear it looked. It is made by slowly melting unsalted butter, which evaporates most of the water content. With the water removed, the milk solids sink to the bottom leaving the golden liquid on top. As you heat the butter, you will want to skim off any surface foam that forms. The resultant liquid should be strained in order to filter out any suspended milk solids. As it cools, the liquid will harden to a solid state just like regular butter. To use it again, just re-warm it over a hot water bath. Clarified butter is also used to make Hollandaise sauce because the water content present in regular butter will change the consistency of the sauce enough to ruin it. To make a really fine Hollandaise sauce I recommend attending culinary school since, to this point, it is the most difficult food we have made. Clarified butter does not taste as rich as regular butter, but you will be very pleased with the results you achieve when using it.

For boiled eggs, it's important to bring the raw eggs to room temperature before immersing them in water. They will be less likely to crack. Bring the water to a boil and then reduce it to a simmer. Do not continue to boil the water or the eggs will bump against each other and crack. If you have ever had your egg yolk turn green, it is because the egg has been overcooked. From a chemistry standpoint, it means that you have heated the egg yolk long enough to bring out the sulphur, which then turns it green. Use the following times for boiled eggs and you won't go wrong.

Soft boiled	3-4 minutes
Medium boiled	5-7 minutes
Hard boiled	12-15 minutes

4 Rules for Cooking Eggs

1. Avoid high heat, low temperature is better.
2. Avoid browning, use clarified butter.
3. Don't overcook.
4. Use a non-stick pan.

Remember, your eggs continue to cook when you take them off the heat, so learn to serve them a little earlier. This concept is called "carry over cooking." If you know someone who always over cooks their meat, remind them that you now know about carry over cooking. This means that meat and other items which are hot, continue to hold their heat long after you remove them from the heat source. Unless you do something to cool the food down, like place it in an ice bath, it will continue to cook. Placing your hard boiled eggs in a ice water bath will most likely give you the best darn hard boiled eggs you've ever had.

Our big challenge was the way in which they wanted us to cook our eggs. The French it seems like their scrambled eggs barely cooked. The chef instructors warned us that if we cook them this way in the U.S., our customers will likely send them back. We learned how to make them French style which isn't too bad since carry over cooking gives them a little more heat. I have to admit that they do look a lot nicer on the plate. We also made omelets, French and American style. The instructor demonstrated this by whisking eggs in the bowl like a mad man. This he says prevents seeing any white in the egg when it scrambles. He then pours the eggs into the pan and scrambles them like crazy. After this, he smoothes the eggs out and using a rubber spatula (heat safe), forms a beautiful rolled omelet. The French omelets are cut open on the top of the roll with the ingredients placed right on top. American omelets we learn, are made the same (with the mad man scrambling) and then ingredients are placed inside and the omelet is gently rolled over and onto the plate. It is our job to present one of each style of omelet to the chef (and yes, he does have to be able to tell the difference!)

Our next challenge is to cook eggs sunny side up, over easy and over medium. We've all cooked eggs at home. How hard can it be? Think Cordon Bleu here. These eggs must be flipped using no spatula. This is easy for the sunny side up, but I'm having a little trouble with the others. How many eggs did he say he has for each of us? I'm thinking that I'm going to need a few extra. My first attempt to flip the egg has it nearly landing in my partner's frying pan. My next attempt has it on the floor. I think you get the idea. The chef instructor says not to worry. Just go to the store and buy a case of eggs. Take them home and practice he says.

Next we poached eggs. Have you ever seen those really neat circles that you can place in a frying pan to poach an egg? My recommendation to you is to buy them. You just can't believe how we poach eggs at Cordon Bleu! We take a very large saucepan full of water and when it is boiling we stir rapidly with our spoon to create a vortex. Next, we drop the egg into the vortex and guess what happens? It looks awful, the white starts breaking apart and it looks nothing like those beautiful poached eggs we are used to seeing on our Egg McMuffins.

Try cooking all your fried eggs without a spatula. That means you must flip them using just the pan! It seems that in the world of Cordon Bleu spatulas do not exist, even though a really nice one came with our tool kit. My friend went to the store and purchased a flat of eggs. She proceeded to practice cooking them all. 96 total. After cleaning up, she put them down the garbage shoot at her apartment. The next day there was a sign posted suggesting that people not put rotten eggs down the shoot. She said it smelled for weeks.

In my apartment there was a brand new stove. I flipped eggs until I burned out all four pilot lights and the sparkling new white stove top was yellow. At that point, I decided that I would never be a breakfast chef! That next weekend I took my spatula out of my tool kit and used it to flip eggs. Guess what? It works great!!

FULL-PROOF HOLLANDAISE SAUCE (trust me, I've tried them all)

2 egg yolks
1 tablespoon lemon juice
3 tablespoons unsalted butter, cold cubes
1 stick unsalted butter, clarified and warm
salt and pepper and cayenne to taste

Whisk egg yolks in small saucepan until they become a pale yellow color and increase in volume.
Add lemon juice and cold butter.

Place pan over bain marie (water bath) and turn stove burner to low.
SLOWLY add clarified butter drop by drop while continuing to whisk.
The sauce should become thick.
Now, add seasoning.
Check the flavor. Add more lemon juice if necessary.
Serve immediately.

Uncut - Chapter 7
The Confidence Factor

My chef instructor told me that what you really need to be successful as a chef, is a very high confidence level in yourself. I am learning not to point out my mistakes to him, since sometimes, I get lucky and he doesn't know how I really prepared something. I must say that these instances are very infrequent, and I am amazed at the things he notices and the subtleties he tastes. If I leave out an ingredient, he knows which one, if I cook something faster than I should have or try to take a short cut, he's on to it. It is quite difficult to pull one over on the chef instructors, who, as they put it, are paid for their amazing palettes.

What is interesting, is that for the most part I am left alone at my stove, oven, and workstation to prepare my dishes. It does seem though, that whenever I make a mistake, the chef instructor just happens to be watching. I asked my chef instructor who has been teaching for six years at my school, if he had pretty much seen it all. He said that he absolutely had. I really admire the bravery of the chef instructor's with all the food they must sample each day. I don't think I could taste 16 servings of eggs benedict! Those bites add up. Speaking of the number of students, we don't have nearly as many as we started with at the beginning of the program. Our combined class started with 36 students three weeks ago, and now there are 32. I suspect more will be gone as we approach finals week and turn in our notebooks. Notebooks you say? Oh, that is another story entirely!

The tests and the amount of homework are definitely a factor in eliminating students from our class. Everyone agrees that the amount of work for the class is much more than we ever anticipated. I have told my husband from the beginning of school that I don't care about my grade. When I first decided to go school I gave no consideration to the fact that there EVEN were grades. I was a pretty average student in college, and so it surprised me when I realized that now, suddenly, the grade did matter to me. It mattered a great deal. This is why I spent every extra waking moment that I could working on my notebook and studying for the exams. If I missed even one question on a test, I beat myself up for the rest of the week. My husband kept saying "I thought it wasn't about the grade?" To this, I had no response. Clearly, this was just one more example of things that I didn't anticipate about going to culinary school. Grades for practicals (actual cooking) counted too. Every day we receive a daily grade. Does this mean that dishes we really screw up get a zero? No, fortunately it doesn't work that way. The instructors give us a lot of credit for attempting to make something. Whew!

People always seemed to be very surprised to hear that we had homework, let alone tests. I tried to explain to them that this culinary school is serious stuff. They always shook their heads in total surprise. Early on we learned that 'a pint is a pound the world around!' This, the cheerful chef instructor told us, will help you remember that 16 oz. is one lb which is one pint. If that was the only conversion we needed to know! Every single test for every week of school included conversions. Things like how many tablespoons are in a cup? C'mon, chefs I said, who doesn't have a measuring spoon? The first few weeks the conversions were fairly simple and then they continued to increase in difficulty. How many ounces in a gallon? How many teaspoons? How many grams in an ounce. These were word problems at their finest. The grading was tough too. A conversion question was frequently interrelated and so missing portion of it could cause you to miss a whole string of conversions. This could easily lop off 30 points from your weekly quiz grade. Multiple choice questions did not seem to exist at Cordon Bleu. Most of the rest of our quizzes and tests consisted of essay answers to questions such as: list the 14 steps to making a perfect stock (in order). We were also required to know ratios (rather than exact recipes), but all ingredients needed to be listed.

My chef instructor told me yesterday that everything can be fixed. This is a lesson which I carried with me throughout my culinary school career. Yes, I do seem to recall "fixing" my Hollandaise sauce. We are reminded by our instructors that in the industry, food cannot be wasted, so they are teaching me to be frugal and to make things work rather than throw them away. I've also learned that I should use my scrap vegetables (known as trim) to make my stocks, and to make a soup of the day at the end of the week with the things that won't last through the weekend in the refrigerator.

This week, I learned to be creative with quiches, make a no-fail pie crust and roll laminated pasta. I had never heard of laminated pasta until I saw it done. It is truly beautiful, but time consuming. I'm convinced that these chef instructors absolutely do not sleep at night. That is the only way they could ever come up with this crazy stuff they make us do every day. Basically, after pasta is rolled out through a pasta machine, you place the herb leaves of your choice on the dough, fold it over, and roll the pasta again. Now, you have a very attractive "laminated" pasta dough. Fresh pasta cooks much faster than dried, so if you do try your hand at making fresh pasta, remember not to cook it too long or it will become extremely sticky. If you're thinking of the pasta machines that you've seen on television, forget it. They will never be smart enough to make laminated pasta!

I also learned the secrets of cooking rice pilaf and risotto. Risotto is also known as Arborio rice. What makes it special is that it can absorb a lot of liquid and maintain a firmness even after it is fully cooked. The secret to making really good risotto is to add your liquid slowly and let the Arborio cook well in between the additions. Risotto can be prepared with any ingredients that you want, but traditionally it is finished with grated parmesan cheese and butter. It is available to you at the grocery store, so surprise your family one night with this Italian treat. To make it really wonderful, use a homemade stock as your liquid ingredient.

RISOTTO

½ stick unsalted butter
1 large onion cut into brunoise cubes
¼ cup dry, white wine
1 cup Arborio rice
1 quart chicken or vegetable Stock (heated)
Salt and pepper to taste
¼ cup Parmesan or Mascarpone cheese
Butter, unsalted (2 – 3 tablespoons)

Cut onions into beautiful brunoise cubes (1/16" x 1/16" x 1/16"), just like we did at Cordon Bleu!
Sweat the onions in butter, making sure they aren't swimming in it!
Add Arborio rice and stir to coat the rice.
Add a small amount of white wine. (approximately ¼ cup)
Cook until all of the wine is absorbed.
Now begin introducing warm stock slowly.

Two things are important in order to make risotto successfully: 1) You must have hot stock and, 2) You must be patient. You will see that the Arborio rice will probably absorb several cups of stock, but you can't just pour it all in at once as you do when you are making regular rice. Arborio rice needs to absorb the stock slowly.
Cook the Arborio on low-medium heat, adding stock only when the previous stock addition has been almost completely absorbed. The Arborio will eventually begin to soften and will probably be done in about 20-30 minutes.
To test for doneness, place a piece of Arborio on the counter and smash it down with your finger. When it is done, it will be soft and will form three little dots on the countertop.
Finish with salt, pepper, butter and parmesan cheese to taste.
For an interesting variation, substitute mascarpone cheese for the parmesan.

RICE PILAF

Take one cup of short grain white rice and sauté it in 2 tablespoons unsalted butter.

When the rice has taken on a golden color, add two cups of water and three quarter teaspoon kosher salt. Bring to boil, give the rice a stir, cover with lid and then reduce heat to a simmer. Set timer for 20 minutes. Don't look at the rice while it cooks. After 20 minutes remove it from the heat. Wait 10 minutes and fluff rice with fork. Serve immediately.

If you want to make your rice ahead of time you will find that it reheats nicely in the microwave. Of course we didn't have microwaves at school, in case you were wondering! Just place rice in a microwave safe bowl and sprinkle with a few drops of water. Cover with plastic wrap and cook on medium high for 1-2 minutes. Rice will be steaming hot and nobody will know that you prepared it ahead of time.

Patrice Johnson

Uncut - Chapter 8
Finals and Notebooks

It's the end of Introduction to Culinary Arts I, and it is hard to believe that four weeks has gone by so quickly. A few days before the end of this class, we had a special 'restaurant day' where we prepared lasagna and any other items which we wanted to accompany it. We worked together as a team on this project, and the chef instructor gave us the whole morning to put together an entire meal, complete with a printed menu and centerpiece. As we worked, our chef instructors left the room. This was quite a surprise, since they had never done this before. They usually watched us like hawks at all times. I did catch them peering in through the door and watching us work. They had curious smiles on their faces as if they were thinking, "I taught them, and now they don't need me any more. Look at them cooking on their own!" The pride on their faces was obvious. I was thinking that I needed to repeat this class, and that I definitely did still need them! I absolutely couldn't face the thought of starting a new class again next Monday. It was like starting school over again and I was petrified!

The chef instructors told us on the first day of class that they most enjoy teaching this introductory I class because they get to witness people "get it for the first time." The chef instructor came in and visited each of our mock restaurants to eat our meals. From my team, he was impressed with everything, especially our lemon pot de crèmes for dessert. I was especially proud since they were one of my specialties prior to attending school. I really did still know how to cook some things! Maybe my confidence factor was improving.

Now the class is winding down and it is time to turn in our notebooks. These notebooks are bound in 4" binders and consist of all of our class notes, homework, and recipes (as well as typed methods for the recipes). Each page must be placed inside a plastic page protector and all pages must be numbered and correspond with a typed table of contents. The chef instructor has warned us from day one not to wait until the last minute to finish our notebooks, but alas, several students did not heed his advice and stayed up all night trying to put pages in order. They arrived to class the next day exhausted. It was not a good idea, since the notebooks were due the same morning that finals began. On the morning of finals, a few students were missing. The chef instructor suggested that we wait for them, because surely they would be here any minute. It is not recommended that one is late to class, because it equals a huge deduction if you are. After 15 minutes they still had not arrived. The chef instructor went out into the hallway to look for them. Apparently he found them upstairs in the library. They were trying to finish their notebooks and had been up all night. Neither father or son looked very well as they came into the class room to take the written final.

This was the beginning of our Introduction to Culinary I finals which lasted for three days. We were allotted 1½ hours to complete the written portion of the exam. Following the written exam, we had to demonstrate our knife skills. This was really scary to me since I am not yet comfortable making 1/8 x 1/8 x 1/8 perfect cubes! In fact, I'm still down right scared of the knives, which is why I am convinced that I am not going to Intro II yet. YIKES!

For the next 2 ½ days, we were at the mercy of the instructors. We did not know prior to each day what we had to make. They told us each day what to prepare and we had to make it on the spot. We could use no recipe cards or notes of any kind, and there was absolutely no talking at all in the classroom; we were on our own. This was very stressful since we had learned over the course of the last four weeks how to help each other and work as teams. My partner and I looked at each other with nervous eyes. I absolutely couldn't operate the pasta machine without him. He couldn't get organized without me. We were doomed!

Suddenly, the first day was over and now it was a waiting game. I wondered what material I should go home and review. What would they ask us to make for day two? I tried to rationalize that some products are expensive and surely they would not be included. It was all just a guessing game!

Our last day included a very difficult layered dish. The bottom layer was Pommes Anna, basically a nightmare of a potato dish. Potatoes had to be peeled and made as round as possible. Then you had to slice them paper thin and layer them in a circle in a small sauté pan. Each layer stacks on top of the next one with just the smallest of overlap for each potato, thus forming a beautiful pattern. Of course, if you do not get the potatoes sliced thin enough, you will never get them to stack. In addition, after they are finished cooking, the clarified butter should hold them together forming a patty type of potato. If you are lucky, you will be able to flip them over keeping them in one piece. If they fall apart, as mine usually do, you can try your best to patch them back together. Once this has been accomplished, you have the bottom layer of this dish. On top of that was a poached egg topped with creamed spinach and a Hollandaise sauce. I took one look at the instructions for this, our final project and figured that yes, I would be taking this class again! Of everything that we had learned they picked the very things which I absolutely could not do.

The days of final exams went faster than I expected and before I knew it, I was having an exit interview with the chef instructor and receiving my final grade. I received a 92% on my final (which included a dismal 78% for my knife cuts), and a 100% for my notebook. My final grade was a 97%, giving me a 3.8 GPA. I was completely drained, but thrilled. The chef instructor told me that he thought I had a great attitude. I'm really glad he couldn't read my mind. Practicing my confidence level was really paying off!

I smiled and walked out of my first official culinary school class feeling extremely pleased. Now, I thought, I know how much meaning becoming a chef will really have. Immediately I began to think of Introduction to Culinary Arts II and what we would do there. I went shopping for a new notebook.

Patrice Johnson

POACHED SALMON (or any other fish) in a Court Bouillon
Serves 2

Court bouillons are typically made with vinegar or wine.
Poaching fish guidelines are approximately eight minutes for every
    inch of fish.
Court bouillon will provide an excellent and delicate flavor to the fish,
    not to mention that it is easy to prepare.
Court bouillons may also be used to poach vegetables.

3 cups water
3 cups white wine
1-2 large onions, sliced
1 carrot peeled, sliced
1 bouquet garni (Parsley, thyme and bay leaf) tied together or put in a
    piece of cheesecloth bag. By placing herbs in a bag or tying them
    together, it is easy to remove them when you are finished cooking.
¼ teaspoon crushed pepper
2 tablespoons salt
One 8 oz. filet of fish

Combine all ingredients except for fish in a large, deep pot and bring
    to a simmer.
Do not boil. Simmer mixture for about one half hour.
Strain and keep liquid at poaching temperature (160 – 180 degrees).
Place fish in court bouillon making sure that it is completely submerged.
Poach until fish is done (remember this will depend on the size of your
    fillet).
Remove from court bullion and serve.

POACHED SALMON VIN BLANC
Serves 2

8 oz. salmon filet
2 tablespoons butter
2 shallots, chopped fine
¼ cup white wine
1 cup chicken stock (may substitute clam juice)
1 egg yolk and ¼ cup cream (liaison)
salt and pepper to taste
1-2 tablespoons lemon juice or more depending on your preference.

Season both sides of salmon fillet with salt and pepper.
Melt butter in large sauté pan and place shallots in the butter to soften.
Add wine and stock to cover the fish.
Cover with a small round piece of buttered parchment paper.
Bring to simmer. Do not boil.
Cover with lid.
Place fish in a 400° oven for 5 minutes.
Drain poaching liquid into sauté pan.
Reduce until half of the liquid remains (demi-sec)
Strain.
Adjust seasonings. (salt, pepper and lemon juice)
Temper in liaison.
Top with butter.
Coat fish with sauce.

Patrice Johnson

Uncut - Chapter 9
Intro II

It is hard to believe that six weeks of school have passed. With Intro I behind us, it's on to Intro II. In this six week course we will learn how to cook all kinds of meat and fish. We'll also spend time learning some basics about salads, starches and other side dishes. The chef instructors have informed us that Intro II is one of the most stressful and difficult classes at culinary school. Great! Get it over with now, I figure. This could be the end for me, I thought. My friend and I noticed the brand new students arriving to the campus this morning. A new class begins every six weeks. Just seeing them and the looks on their faces made us feel much better. We were on our way! We had made it through six weeks and it sure did fly by!

We began this class with a review of the fire safety system in our classroom and how to avoid starting fires. This must be a major concern here at the school, since we spent about an hour learning what to do, when to evacuate, and when to just close your eyes.

The Ansul fire system will go off if something gets too hot under the hoods over the stoves. The chef instructor warns that it will release a white powder, which will disperse over the stoves first, then the remainder of the kitchen. It will almost always put out a fire. It will also close down the kitchen and the school for the rest of the day, so the instructor has asked us to please try to keep our fires small. "You bet, Chef!" I say under my breath to my partner.

What is the major difference between this class and Intro I? Time and plating components. All dishes are now timed, and they consist of an entire meal, not just one item. Each plate must have a protein, a starch, a vegetable, a sauce, and a garnish. In addition, everything must be centered perfectly on the plate with nothing touching the rim. The plate must be at the right temperature for the food item being served, perfectly clean and, most importantly, on time!

The other fun and new element of the class was that we would now enjoy having a mystery box to complete once a week. Mystery boxes entailed a surprise of sorts. It works like this. On the given morning of a mystery box, the instructor gives you a few ingredients and you have to take these items, add other appropriate ingredients, and create a stunning, tasty, and beautiful meal. Mystery boxes sound absolutely horrible to me. I am used to cooking with a recipe and I'm thinking that there is no way that I am going to make something without having a chance to spend at least a week thinking about it. One of the first mystery box items that we receive is a butternut squash. Simple, I think! Just make the butternut squash soup you made in Intro I. I did, and it was a huge success. This doesn't mean I'm feeling any more confident about mystery boxes, but I am learning that I can cook without doing all of the planning and recipe reading which I used to do prior to coming to school.

Meanwhile, our science lab experiments are continuing. As part of the daily demonstration, our chef places some broccoli in a pot of boiling water. He then adds some vinegar which turns the broccoli into an ugly olive green color. He reminds us that of course everything can be fixed. He adds some baking soda to the water and the vegetables turn bright green. Next he takes some red cabbage places it in boiling water and adds baking soda. The color basically goes away, leaving the cabbage looking pale and bleached out. Before we can say oooh, he throws some vinegar into the pot and the cabbage instantly turns into a bright red as we say ahhhh. Turns out that these chemical reactions differ depending on what type of pigment you are dealing with. Also turns out that there is a large list of the various pigments as well as the effects of acid and alkaline on them. We'll get to know it well since it appears on tests on a regular basis.

We are going to work with emulsions again, which after Hollandaise sauce are one of my least favorite things at school. Today, we're going to make Caesar salad. The chef instructor shows us the secret of whisking the egg yolks and slowly adding the olive oil. Alas, when we try it back at our work stations, the dressing is not getting thick like his was.

I decide that I probably have a bad egg yolk, so I throw it away and begin again. Now you and I have been making Caesar salad at home for years. I mean, it is simple with a blender, right? You simply throw everything in and hit the on button. Blenders of course, are not available at Cordon Bleu! At home you probably have added some grated parmesan to your salad. No way! We're making parmesan fricos to go with the Caesar. Basically, you take some parmesan cheese and grate it. Then you place it in the bottom of a small sauté pan and melt it. When you take it off the stove, you immediately mold the cheese over a small ramekin; thus forming a parmesan frico. The idea is to have them fairly thin, but the thinner they are, the more chance you have of breaking them as you place them over the ramekin or better yet try to remove them from the ramekin. After several attempts, my frico looks pretty freaky and I try to hide it under the lettuce leaves of my Caesar. Caesar salad, I can tell, is one that I will have to work very hard on!

During our first exercise at this new and fun way to cook, I was proud to get my first dish done close to the deadline. As I tried to wipe the plate clean, it seemed that I was just making it worse. Trying to prioritize in my mind, I decided to forget about the cleanliness of the plate and worry about my food, which was getting cold. Surely the food was more important, right? I proudly took my first dish up to the instructor's desk. Someone else was there already, but this wouldn't impact my time too much, would it? The instructor noted immediately when I put the plate down that I was four minutes late. Imagine, four minutes! I was thrilled to have completed the dish at all! I also wanted to point out that I had to wait about 30 seconds behind someone else, but I thought better of it.

Patrice Johnson

The next comment out of the chef instructor's mouth was that he thought he was going to fall off of his chair. He leaned way over to one side on his stool. I did not understand his humor, but I quickly learned that he had a problem with my food not being perfectly centered. Next, he pointed out that the plate was very streaky. "Yes, Chef", I said. One thing I have learned is that you do not argue with the chef instructors because they have an answer for everything! They are also always right! Having learned this lesson well by the end of Intro I, I listened respectfully to the many other comments he had about the various items on the dish. I almost laughed when he added "good job, Patrice" as an afterthought. Welcome to Intro II. I decided on the first day that I was going to hate this class!

CLASSIC CAESAR SALAD DRESSING

3 egg yolks
5 anchovy filets, chopped fine (optional)
2 tsp. minced fresh garlic
2 tsp. Dijon mustard
1 oz. red wine vinegar
salt and pepper to taste
1 teaspoon. Tabasco and Worcestershire
1 tablespoon lemon juice (or to your taste preference)
1 ½ - 2 cups virgin olive oil
2 tablespoons parmesan cheese
Croutons (recipe below).

Mix the anchovy filet and the garlic together to make into a paste like mixture.
The original classic version of Caesar did not contain anchovy, so don't feel bad if you leave it out.
Whisk egg yolks, Dijon mustard, vinegar together. If you are mixing by hand it will take a few minutes to achieve a nice thick base.
When the mixture is thick, slowly drizzle in olive oil.
Add Tabasco, Worcestershire, lemon, salt and pepper.
Remember that each egg yolk can absorb up to 8 oz. of olive oil.
The secret to getting the dressing thick is to really beat that egg yolk well before you start adding the oil.
Rinse and dry romaine lettuce leaves.

Take the 2 tablespoons of grated parmesan cheese and melt it in an
ungreased non-stick pan. While the cheese is still hot, take it out
of the pan with a spatula and immediately form it into a cup shape
using a small ramekin as a guide.

Serve your salad on a very cold plate with the parmesan frico and
home made croutons.

CROUTONS:

Slice French bread into thin slices.
Drizzle with olive oil, salt and pepper and bake until lightly toasted.

Patrice Johnson

Uncut - Chapter 10
Chicken and more Chicken

This week we are learning how to fabricate a chicken. Fabricate means to cut it into its various parts. Why don't they just say cut it up? Because it's culinary school! We are finding that there is a whole new language to learn.

Our chef instructors ordered sixty chickens; two for each of us. We reviewed sanitation skills since chicken tends to be a prime contributor to food poisoning. The chef instructors told us to assume that every chicken has salmonella on it and to treat it and our preparation areas with great care. "We do not want to get sick this term", they warned! Apparently last term they were sick from food poisoning each and every week for six straight weeks. They are not exactly in good moods regarding this topic and who can blame them? One of the things that they stressed was to stop wiping our hands on our side towels, which we hang off our aprons. This is something we have been doing routinely for four weeks, so it is difficult now to un-learn. We were also reminded to thoroughly clean with bleach our cutting board, knives, and work table before chopping any vegetables on it. They informed us that they will be watching us like hawks and deducting points from our daily grade should be decide not to comply with the sanitation rules.

After we cut the chickens into various pieces (leg, thigh, breast and wing), we learned how to remove the bones from them. We also learned how to french the bone, which means to peel the fat and meat away from the bone so most of the bone is exposed. This makes the final presentation fancier and it is becoming quite popular in the gourmet cooking world. I'm amazed that I cut the chicken up. I've always enjoyed buying those nice packages of chicken already cut up at the store!

We made some really neat lollipop drumsticks with the bone frenched and sticking straight up in the air. We will use them in our Coq au Vin, a traditional dish of dark chicken meat braised to make it more tender. Braising is a technique where you begin cooking on the stovetop and finish it in the oven. When braising, liquid must cover your product 2/3 of the way up. For this dish, the liquid is burgundy wine. After the entire class had made drumstick lollipops, we put them into a large vat that the instructor then filled with burgundy wine and mirepoix (carrots, onions and celery) which together form the braising liquid. This meat/liquid mixture will soak overnight. The next day we are ready for the final preparations of the dish. We sear the chicken with hot oil in a sauté pan. Then, to complete the dish, we make a pan sauce using the braising liquid.

We now make pan sauces daily. Are they difficult? Absolutely! They are definitely tricky. Let's make a pan sauce Le Cordon Bleu style. Remove your meat from the pan you cooked it in and keep it warm. Remove most of the fat from your pan by pouring it off. Add onions or shallots and cook them until soft, but do not brown them. Deglaze the pan with wine (take your pan off of the heat when adding the wine). Add stock, or your braising liquid, and simmer until the sauce begins to thicken. Strain sauce and check for seasoning. Here's the tricky part: swirl in butter while the pan is still off the heat. Note that the butter should be very cold as you swirl it in. The more butter you add, the thicker it will make your sauce. What if you get it too thick? You can always thin it down with stock. If you are careful, the butter will thicken the sauce and make it very shiny. Even if you are careful, the butter may separate and your sauce will "break". I'm starting to wonder if we will we ever get away from these emulsions! Easy answer: No! Now add the sauce to your meat, and do remember to keep it centered on your plate!

Try making some pan sauces. I think you will be impressed by how nice they look on your meat and how wonderful they taste. Don't be afraid of them as I was. The more you practice making them the easier they will become. Trust me!

COQ AU VIN CHICKEN
Serves 4

The recipe for Coq au Vin chicken is from the Burgundy region of France and is classically made using Burgundy wine. It was in the olden days made from an old rooster which typically had tough meat. Classic garnishes for the dish are bacon, mushrooms and onions. Even more classic garnishes are the cock's cone and kidney. That may be more than your guests are ready for!

8 chicken legs and thighs marinated overnight in burgundy wine
2 large white onions, small diced, marinated as above
2 carrots, small diced, marinated as above
1 celery rib, small diced marinated as above
2 garlic cloves, minced
½ cup. brandy
3 cups burgundy wine (reserved from marinade)
1 cup chicken stock
Salt and pepper to taste
Bouquet garni (Parsley, Thyme & Bay leaf tied together or placed in cheesecloth)
4 bacon strips cut into slices
10 pearl onions
5-7 mushrooms, cut in half
Beurre manie for thickening (made from 2 tablespoons flour, 2 tablespoons softened unsalted butter and mixed into a paste).

Begin by marinating chicken and vegetables in a large container over night.
In a large sauté pan sauté bacon until chewy. Reserve for garnish.
Blanch pearl onions in boiling water until tender, place immediately in ice bath, drain and peel.
Sauté pearl onions and mushrooms until golden.

Brown marinated mirepoix (this is your carrot, celery and onion which have been marinating). Brown until golden brown and caramelized. Add garlic, taking care not to burn it.

Add brandy to pan and continue to cook until most of the liquid has been reduced.

Add wine and cook until mixture is reduced by one half.

Pour liquid into a large Dutch oven with chicken stock, salt and pepper and bouquet garni.

Brown marinated chicken in saucepan in fat or oil on high heat.

Turn once.

When chicken has been browned, remove from sauté pan and place into Dutch oven.

Cover and place in a 325 degree oven and cook for 30-45 minutes or until tender.

Remove chicken and keep it warm.

Strain sauce in pan and then return sauce to heat.

Add beurre manie slowly and whisking until it has dissolved.

This will thicken the sauce.

Add reserved bacon, onion and mushroom garnish to sauce.

Taste for seasoning and add salt and pepper if necessary.

Serve immediately.

MAPLE GLAZED CARROTS
Serves 4

2 tablespoons unsalted butter
1/4 cup pure maple syrup
1/4 cup water
salt and pepper
6 large carrots

Peel carrots and slice into 1" thick diagonal slices.

Melt butter in large frying pan.

Sauté carrots in butter.

Add salt and pepper to taste

Add water and bring to boil.

Reduce heat and add maple syrup.

Cook 4-8 minutes or until carrots are only slightly soft and are glazed with the maple sauce.

Uncut - Chapter 11
Here's The Beef

We spent one entire week cooking and eating all types of beef. Beef being my favorite food, I was in hog heaven (no pun intended here). Filet mignon for breakfast; not a good habit to start, but I did. We learned to cook beef in a pan, in the oven, and on the grill. Grilling, it seems, is much more complex than I ever thought. Not that I had ever done any grilling prior to school. That task had always been assigned to my husband for nights that I wanted to take off. The steak must be positioned on the grill at 10 o'clock (the position, not the time of day). There it sears for about two minutes and is then moved to the 2 o'clock position, but not turned over. After you have cooked the steak for another two minutes, it is turned over and the process is repeated (10 o'clock, then 2 o'clock). Turning times vary depending on how the steak is to be cooked. The 10:00-2:00 method makes the perfect hatch marks on the steak, supposedly. Fortunately for me, we were covering the steak with a nice thick sauce, so my hatch marks, such as they were, were not too noticeable.

It would be way too easy to just cook a filet mignon to the required temperature. Today, we have a greater challenge. We are going to make a sauce for the filet, grill it and then serve it stacked with a piece of foie gras on top. Oh, the ever popular foie gras! Is it good and do I feel sorry for the geese are the questions everyone wanted to know. Let's talk liver in general. Prior to cooking foie gras, which is fatted goose liver, we cooked regular beef liver. The chef instructors assured us that this was not the liver we remembered from our childhood and they encouraged us all to try it. The smell of liver cooking in my household as a child usually drove me directly out of the house. When I smelled the first piece of liver being seared, it was exactly reminiscent of my childhood liver memories. I took my cooked liver up to the instructor who told me it was cooked well and that I should definitely taste it. I took it directly to the trash can. The smell of it was enough for me. So, I have to tell you, that the thought of tasting the foie gras was very unappealing to me. I asked the instructor "Why in the world does one need foie gras when you have the very best beef to eat?" He said, "Try it, and you'll see why." Given the price of foie gras averages $50 per pound, I figured I should definitely get my money's worth, so I gave it a try. I would have to describe it as very buttery in flavor and not at all like the traditional beef liver. It also doesn't have the odor that beef liver does. Not too bad, but I still didn't think the filet needed it. Foie gras it seemed to me was not something I needed to try again. I had no idea how often I would see it throughout school (and I'm glad that I didn't know then!). I actually grew fond of this delicacy before my school days ended.

Beef we learned is quality graded. Frequently you will see beef marked with a sticker that says USDA. This represents the grade of the beef. Use of meat grading services is voluntary, however only the Meat Grading and Certification Branch of the USDA can apply the official grade marks. The top grade is Prime, then Choice, and finally Select. Most of us buying beef in our local grocery store will be getting Select. Prime and Choice go to the restaurants. If you have a chance to buy Choice or Prime, do so. You will be able to tell the difference. The degree of marbling in beef is what determines how the beef is graded. Marbling is considered to be a good thing, so the more marbling, the higher the grade.

I never imagined that we would make hamburgers at school, but we did. They were very good and the instructor was quick to point out why. Here is how to fashion hamburgers Le Cordon Bleu style: 75% meat with 25% additional pork fat added to the lean ground beef. The chef instructor says you can't have a really good low fat hamburger. This is a fact: nobody is watching fat content at Le Cordon Bleu. I know if you are like me, you have always spent time searching for the lowest fat beef with which to make your hamburgers. I have to admit though that adding pork fat does give them a fabulous flavor!

We learned how to make our own French fries to go with the hamburgers. There is nothing better than fresh home made French fries. The chef instructors have waited a few weeks before letting us near the huge deep fat fryers, but now we turn them on each day along with our stoves and ovens. One day while cooking on the stove, a particularly nervous student's pan began to swirl off the stove. The pan was full of hot oil and had caught fire. It was heading towards the deep fat fryer. She was in a panic and others around here weren't thinking clearly either. The chef instructor stepped in just in time to catch the pan before it hit the deep fat fryer. Had it done so, we probably would have had the chance to witness the Ansul fire system at work. The chef instructor told us of a student who had his toque catch on fire. Rather than remaining calm, he ran out of the classroom which fanned the fire on his toque, thus making the flames larger. The instructor told us that they never saw that student again. He did not even return for his personal items!

The most tender part of beef we learn is the tenderloin. It is also the part of beef that is considered to have the least amount of flavor. That is why you frequently see bacon wrapped filet mignons. Chuck and round steak have the most flavor, but they must be tenderized before cooking. For this reason, these types of beef are best suited to marinades. Flank steak comes from the belly of the cow and is not tender. If you cook a marinated flank steak, it must be cooked to a temperature of medium rare, otherwise it will get too tough. Don't even think about cooking flank steak that has not been marinated.

Speaking of marinades, let me share a nice one with you. These quantities are for every pound of flank (or round) steak.

Patrice Johnson

MARINATED FLANK STEAK

2 garlic cloves
¼ cup soy sauce
¼ cup sugar
1/8 cup sesame oil
1/8 cup dry sherry
1 teaspoon fresh ginger, grated
½ tsp. coarse ground black pepper.

Combine all ingredients and coat your steak with the marinade for as long as you can. Overnight is ideal. Remember to turn the meat periodically. Now, here's a culinary school tip: after removing the steak from the marinade, pat it dry. The reason for this must remain secret (another way of saying "nobody knows for sure why, it just works"). Season with salt and pepper. Run an oiled rag across your grill so the steak doesn't stick. Grill your beef. Please, I want to see those hatch marks at 10 and 2 o'clock!

While your steak is grilling, strain your marinade mixture into a sauce pan. Heat over medium-low heat to reduce the sauce. Now you have a nice glaze for your meat. This is really handy if you don't get those hatch marks just right!

Keep in mind that you may never use your beef marinade without boiling it since raw beef has been in contact with the marinade juices.

Enjoy!

Uncut - Chapter 12
Family Day

Now that we are "experts" at cooking beef we have moved on to pork. Pork, it so happens, is one of the safest meats in this country today. It has to be cooked well done though, right? Wrong! There hasn't been an outbreak of trichinosis in this country since 1948, but as the chef instructor pointed out, everyone is overcooking their pork. This dries it out and it loses its flavor. He warned us that if we cook our pork properly (i.e., still showing some pink) some customers will send it back assuming it hasn't been thoroughly cooked. I'm afraid I'm guilty of the same mistake. I've sent my husband back to the grill many times with what I now realize were perfectly cooked pork chops. Do not be afraid to cook your pork with some pink in the middle. Cook the pork to 145° F and I think you will be in for a real treat. Remember that your carry over cooking concept will continue to cook the pork after you take it off the grill. Keeping this in mind really helps to not over cook the meat and dry it out.

Remember carry over cooking? It is what happens when you cook something and then take it off the heat: it continues to cook. This is why a steak or roast that is medium rare when removed from the heat, will, by the time you slice it, be medium or medium well done. You must allow for carry over cooking. The larger the item, the more carry over cooking there will be.

Despite our paradigms about pigs, it appears that they are one of the cleanest animals. Who knew? There is less chance of bacteria in pork than from beef or chicken. See what kind of expertise you can impress your friends with when you go to culinary school?

Today is my turn to be the daily sous chef. What does this mean? Well, it means that I have a lot of extra work to do in addition to getting all of my daily products cooked. Usually the sous chef is at the beck and call of the chef instructor all day. The idea here is to simulate the role of the sous chef in the real world. The sous chef is usually next in command after the head chef. Today, I am gathering a team of others together so that we can make stock. We are going to make 30 gallons each of veal stock, chicken stock, white veal stock and fish stock. This requires chopping tons of vegetables for our mirepoix, and we are all eager to get the stocks "up", which means put them on the stove to simmer. Once this is done we will be free to go work for a while. It will still be our job to keep an eye on the stocks all day to make sure that they do not boil.

At the end of the day we will "drop the stock" which means that we will take if off the stoves, strain it and stir it with a large ice Popsicle-like stick to cool it down. I will not be able to leave for the day until the stock has been properly stored in the huge walk in refrigerator across the hall from our classroom. We will label the stock and hope that other classes do not steal it since we know that it is far superior to other classes stocks.

By the time that we get back to our work stations, we find that we are already way behind the other students and now we need to get caught up. Most of us dread the day that we have to be the sous chef for this very reason. Fortunately these duties only come around about once every six week class. My partner usually gives me a hand on these days and today he sneaks me some perfectly cubed mirepoix for one of my sauces. I am relieved to know that maybe now I have half a chance of completing the days dishes on time!

The excitement level is high today in the classroom because we are having family day at the school tomorrow. This means that we have been allowed to invite members of our family to come for lunch. We are going to work as teams to prepare the various food items which we will serve and pork ribs will be the highlight of the meal.

Because we spent this week focusing on learning the primal cuts of pork, we have a lot of good lunch time conversation pieces ready. For example, primal basically means the different sections of the animal beginning with the front of the animal. Meat roasts and ribs come from the primals. It was fascinating learning and memorizing these primal cuts. On our test this week we had to sketch the pig and show where the primals are located. First, let's talk about the loin primal, which is where these luscious ribs are coming from. Ribs come in three varieties: Baby back, St. Louis, and Spare Ribs. Baby back ribs are from the top of the rib cage, St. Louis come from the middle, and Spare from the bottom. Yes, I know what you're thinking. I was feeling my own ribs trying to picture this too while in class! While baby back ribs are touted frequently on restaurant menus, it is really the spare ribs that have less bone and the most meat on them. These are the ribs that we plan to serve for our family members.

The beginning of the next day started out very smoothly. One team prepared side dishes to go with the ribs. We also cooked chicken and jalapeno pepper poppers which we deep fried. A dessert team had prepared lots of goodies, including my very own famous Butterfinger cheesecake. The Baking I instructor showed up with a large platter of cookies which we proudly arranged with our other desserts. The only real catastrophe so far had been the black olives we put in our pasta salad. A student came over to taste it and found that they had pits in them. This, I never lived down for the rest of school, but we picked out every olive and pitted it! To this day I only buy pitted olives.

Our guests were due to arrive at 12:00 noon and we arranged the long steel preparation tables in rows with our stools for our family members to sit down. Everyone was beaming. The instructors warned us gravely at 11:45 that we had better hurry since we didn't have much time.

We told the chef's that we were ready to go, everything was actually ready ahead of schedule. Looking out into the hallway, we noticed some of family members were already here. They were peering into the windows; very curious to see this place that we had tried to describe to them. The chef instructor told us to begin letting everyone in and that is when the fire alarm began to go off. I had never in my 9 weeks of school heard the fire alarm and it was ear piercing to say the least. All of us looked at each other in horror and then ran to get our knife kits. If the school was going to burn up, at least we'd leave with our knife kits intact.

I told my partner that I was absolutely sure it was just a false alarm as we headed to the first floor and out to the sidewalk in front of the school. This was when the fire trucks pulled up. It was high noon. In addition to all of the students standing out on the sidewalk watching the firemen race into the building, all of our family members were also there. "Why, oh why did this have to happen today, of all days?" I asked my friend.

I kept hoping that the ansel fire system hadn't been set off because that meant the school would be closed for the rest of the day. In a few minutes we were all allowed back into the school and learned that an Intro I student had simply burned a roux. Oh brother, we thought, we couldn't comprehend someone burning a roux. Why four weeks ago when we were in Intro I, we were roux experts. Now, as Intro II students we felt much superior to those silly Intro I students and not only that, they had almost spoiled our special family day! As it turned out our families had a wonderful time and the food was pretty good too. The poppers were a huge success as were the deep fried candy bars that we served for dessert.

I know your mouths are watering now, so I won't hold back on the rib recipe and how to wow your friends at the next cookout. It wouldn't be fair not to share deep fried candy bars too.

GRILLED RIBS

Begin with 3 pounds pork ribs, your choice (Baby back, St. Louis or
    Spare).

Dry rub:
¼ cup chili powder (New Mexico chili powder)
2 Tablespoons Lawry's seasoned garlic salt
¼ cup paprika (Hungarian)
1/3 cup cumin seed, toasted and ground
2-3 tablespoons kosher salt

Glaze
3 cup garlic, minced Yes, it's okay to use the stuff already minced for
    you in the jar! (no, we weren't allowed to at school!)
2-4 Serrano chilies, chopped
2 tablespoons ground cumin
1 cup lime juice, fresh (squeeze them, don't buy juice in the bottle)
Pinch of salt
3/4 cup honey (or to taste)

Combine all dry ingredients and rub onto both sides of the ribs. Place
    the ribs onto a rack and then place the rack onto top of a baking
    pan. Fill the pan with water ½ way up and cover the ribs with foil.
    Let them bake (steam) for 45 minutes in a 350ºF oven. Don't worry
    if all of the water evaporates. The dry rub will infuse flavor into the
    ribs as they cook.
Combine garlic, jalapeno and cumin in a food processor. Add the lime
    juice and salt and puree.

In a saucepan, add the puree and honey. Bring to a simmer and stir
    constantly so the honey doesn't burn. Reduce sauce to a glaze.
Remove the ribs from the oven and spoon the honey glaze over the
    ribs.
Fire up your grill and heat the ribs on the grill. (At this point they are
    basically already cooked. You are just going to add flavor of the
    honey glaze).

They are absolutely delicious!

Patrice Johnson

DEEP FRIED CANDY BARS

Take your favorite candy bar. Mine of course is Butterfinger.
Bread the candy bar by dipping it in milk and then bread crumbs.
Deep fry it in oil until it gets golden brown.

The chocolate will melt inside the bread coating.
A step above S'mores!

Uncut - Chapter 13
One Fish, Two Fish

It is week three of Intro II and my hands and arms are bruised, burned, blistered, and my hands are aching all the time! Yes, the battle scars of a want-to-be chef are accumulating and some of them are rather ugly! The most dangerous burn in the kitchen is from steam heat. Fortunately, none of my burns are from steam, just grabbing hot pot and pan handles while rushing to present dishes on time. Keep in mind that our pot handles are not insulated like the ones in your kitchen, and no oven mitts are provided either. We have to use our side towels. When the towels get wet they cause the heat to burn you even faster. Everyone reminds me that they explain all of this when you sign up for school. These are the risks of becoming a chef. Gee, I don't remember that explanation on my school tour! I just remember the fascination of the big, beautiful professional kitchens!

The instructors post the times that our plates are due to be presented to them on a white board each morning after the demo. It is after seeing this, that many folks decide that they aren't feeling well and decide to go home for the day. Once this week I was lucky enough to have two complete plates due five minutes apart! This was quite tricky, let me tell you, but I managed to pull it off surprising myself and I think the chef instructor too! The first thing he said was, "Wow, you're on time! Now, go get your other plate." "Boy, I wish I could have this challenge every day", I said sarcastically to my partner as I came back to my work station to pick up plate # 2 which he thankfully was wiping clean for me.

For the past week and half we have been learning to filet and cook fish. We have filleted trout, salmon and catfish. We poached salmon, grilled halibut, and learned some very interesting ways to steam other fish, both in the oven and on the stove top. I snap pictures of the fish while they are still whole, thinking that this is going to really add a lot to my notebook. When I look back at these pictures later, I'm not so sure it was a great idea! Needless to say, I am longing for those filet mignons!

Everyone knows that fish is definitely not at its freshest on Mondays. The same is true at school. On this particular Monday we are in the process of learning how to filet a flounder. These flounder do not meet the criteria of what we have learned about fish being fresh. In fact, they look pretty bad and they smell even worse. Upon making the first cut into mine, I find myself gagging. This is definitely the most gross fish that we have seen. Its insides seem particularly bloody and it smells even worse. About the time I started to gag, one of our class mates yells out from the back of the room "Hey, mine has worms in it. Really cool!" I don't know what I was thinking as I followed my partner over to the other student's workstation. I was picturing a small worm, so I was rather unprepared to see several long earthworms crawling along his cutting board. As I shook my head and fought back vomit in my throat, my partner assured me that I could definitely return to my cutting board and finish filleting my flounder. I looked at her in horror. There is no way that I can prepare this flounder! The chef instructor thinks differently though, so I head back to my station to do my very best to finish cutting up that disgusting fish. This day marked a momentous occasion at school. We had achieved a new level. Whenever things got difficult, my partner and I would comment "I'm at the flounder level!" This saying we carried with us throughout our days at school.

There are three different types of fish: flat, round, and non-bony. All three types can be found in both fresh and salt water. You all have likely seen trout swimming in mountain streams. Trout are round fish. When filleted they produce two filets, one down each side of the fish. Some other common round fish are salmon, perch, and grouper. Flat fish can be divided into four filets. Some examples of flat fish are halibut, flounder and sole. Monkfish is an example of a non-bony fish and is also known as the poor man's lobster. When I tasted the monkfish, I thought it must have been a real poor man because I couldn't even get a hint of the lobster flavor.

Speaking of lobster, we dealt first hand with some live ones. The chef instructors demonstrated how to cook them and promised that in our more advanced classes, we would also have that same opportunity. Gee, I can hardly wait! The instructor had a great deal of fun with our class telling us that sometimes lobsters scream when put into the pot. As he put the second one in the pot it made a horrible scream. My cooking partner and I looked at each other in horror. Seeing we were on the verge of tears, the other chef instructor quickly assured us that, in fact, lobsters don't make any screaming noises, but that sometimes chef instructors do! At this point, I'm thinking my expensive lobster habit may have just gone by the wayside!

We used the lobster to make a lobster ravioli with a very rich sauce. I gave mine to the dish washer who looked at me with unbelieving eyes! None of the other students had parted with their lobster ravioli so he was quite thrilled. I had seen enough lobster for today.

This week we also got to deal with whole catfish. I have never eaten catfish and after seeing one I wasn't ready to taste it. They are quite large to deal with (about the size of a kitty cat), and for some reason much more bloody than the other fish we have had to cut up. They have extremely sharp whiskers which we have to take care not to scratch ourselves with as we prepare to cut its head off. I am not doing well with the fish filleting and I feel very inadequate using my boning knife. I told my friend that there was absolutely no way I could cut the head off of this fish. She assured me that I could and so we both simultaneously whacked its head off and rushed over to the trash can to throw it away. Our entire workstation was covered with the blood of the catfish and folks this just isn't real appetizing if you know what I mean. We took great care to clean everything up and then cut the catfish into filets. Mine were really ugly filets since I had butchered the poor fish rather than gently using my boning knife to take short and small cuts to separate the skin from the meat. I was in a hurry to get it finished and figured that when I rolled the filets up and stuffed them with the mixture of crayfish and ham and topped them with a tomato garlic cream sauce, nobody would be able to tell how bad they really looked.

Meanwhile, as the chef instructor told us how yummy the catfish would be, I was practically gagging. Learning that it was a bottom dweller didn't do much to increase my appetite. Once we served the finished product and the chef instructor encouraged me to try it, I told him that I had to pass. While others said it was tasty, one girl who had tried it went directly to the restroom to lose her catfish lunch. Now, I was even happier about not sampling it. My appetite was pretty much history for the rest of the day.

How to Check for Freshness of a Fish:

Firm Flesh	It should be resilient to the touch.
Eyes	Clear, not cloudy. Should not look sunken in their head.
Gills	Should be red.
Odor	Fish should not smell. If it does have a smell, it should smell like the ocean. It should not have a chemical or ammonia smell.
Belly Burn	Sometimes flesh is eaten away due to the adrenaline a fish has in its system when being caught.

My favorite fish preparation:
Serves 2

Two 6 oz. Halibut, Mahi Mahi or Grouper filets
1 tablespoon extra virgin olive oil
Lemon pepper to taste
¼ cup dry white wine
2 shallots, finely chopped
1/8 cup white wine vinegar.

Rub fish with olive oil and season with salt and pepper or lemon pepper.
Grill fish and keep warm.
In a small sauté pan, combine white wine, finely chopped shallots, and vinegar.

Reduce this mixture until only about 1-2 tablespoons of liquid are left.
Swirl in cold butter, a few pieces at a time.
Add lemon juice to taste.
Season with salt and pepper.

It is yummy and relatively healthy too!

CITRUS MAHI MAHI
Serves 2

½ cup orange juice
½ cup grapefruit juice
¼ cup lemon or key lime juice (fresh)
¾ cup dry sherry
3 tablespoons ginger root, minced
1/3 cup soy sauce
2 tablespoons sesame oil
salt and cayenne pepper to taste
1 teaspoon Hungarian paprika
2 mahi mahi filets (approximately 6 oz. each)

Mix together all juices, sherry, soy sauce, ginger, sesame oil, cayenne
    and salt.
Marinate mahi mahi in the refrigerator for 2-4 hours.

Using a hot, oiled grill cook the mahi mahi.
If you don't have a grill, you can easily broil this fish.
Serve with lemon or lime wedge.

Patrice Johnson

Uncut - Chapter 14
Veal & Lamb

This week the chef instructors had a special treat for us; the fabrication of a whole lamb. They brought him in covered by a sheet. I'm happy to report that he did not have wool anymore, nor did he have a head. Actually, he looked like what you might imagine a large, skinned dog would.

The instructor fabricated (cut) the lamb into all of the major primal parts. This took over an hour and definitely required some real physical stamina. The notable observation about the fabrication is that lambs don't have much meat on them. Now you can understand the high price of lamb on restaurant menus. I didn't eat lamb prior to attending school, but this was really the finale for me. It definitely provided much more information that I needed to have about lamb.

Fortunately, we did not see the fabrication of a calf for our veal lessons. Veal is a very lean meat and is prized for its tenderness. The lack of iron in the calves diet is what produces the white meat of veal. I'm just going to leave it at that.

Every day we have two full plates to complete. At the start of our day everyone runs around the kitchen carrying a sheet pan and gathering up what they will need. The idea in French cooking is to misenplace ("everything in its place") before one actually starts cooking. This, will make the actual cooking much easier. It is usually around this time that people have a look of panic in their eyes. My partner and I usually split up what needs to be gathered and we got it down to a system of what we need and who gets what. We quickly rush over to the stove and place a piece of tape with our names on it to mark our space. This we find, becomes less critical as more weeks go by and there are plenty of stoves available.

On one particular day, the demo lecture was still ongoing and one anxious student kept edging her way over to the stove hoping the instructor wouldn't notice her. Every so often she would place a pot or a pan down hoping that for once she wouldn't be running behind schedule. The chef instructors began to take notice of this advance set up and told us to sit tight until the lecture was over. They assured us that we had plenty of time to get everything in place AFTER the lecture. We of course knew that this was not true.

The next day we had a substitute teacher. On this morning we were all going to make carrot mashed potatoes to go with one of our entrees. This required two separate pots each full of water. One would have potatoes and one carrots. They would be combined together after they were cooked to make a beautiful orange colored mashed potato. The over-anxious student put her potatoes and carrots on to boil before the lecture started, hoping to get a head start on the extensive menus for the day. Long after the lecture, the potatoes and the carrots, dried out and blackened, were found by the substitute instructor. They were stuck to the bottom of the pan and not a bit of water was left in the pots. For all her efforts, the instructor never could get anyone to claim those two blackened pots and the poor disillusioned and frustrated student innocently went to get some more carrots and potatoes to start over. The fear of screwing up was just too much for most of us.

Another student was always the first to be completed with her product. She ran around the kitchen diligently each day, her focus mostly on completing her menu items quickly. Nearly every other day she dropped and broke something on the floor, this most likely due to her haste. Many of us felt sorry for her, because she was very well intentioned, but one student whose patience was beginning to wear thin began to routinely call out as items fell and broke "We need a clean up on aisle one." This produced howls of laughter from the rest of us, but she either never heard him or pretended not to. The rest of us always helped her to clean up the mess and get her back on track again. I had to laugh when we started this class and the instructor asked us to inventory the number of plates we had. We all knew that we would have much less at the end of our six weeks.

While learning about veal and lamb we made a Maitre d'Hotel butter, which can be used for any type of meat. It is a nice butter to make ahead of time and keep in your freezer. Then, when you are ready to serve a steak or a piece of veal, slice the butter and plate it on top of the meat. This will create a nice sauce in lieu of making a pan sauce. It is also convenient because it is something that you can have prepared ahead of time.

Have you ever wondered who washes all of the dishes? Well, here's the best part, we, the students do our own dishes with the exception of pots and pans, for which we are most fortunate to have dishwashers (of the human variety). Now, I'm wondering how they manage to have no students doing dishes when you come through on your tour? Nope, nobody said anything to me about washing dishes. I didn't even wash dishes at home!

At school we wash our dishes using a three part sink method and do not have conveniences like garbage disposers. However, they do have sprayers. For those of you reading at home, I recommend sticking with the automatic dishwashers! (or a spouse who is willing to clean up after you cook!)

Each student is assigned a different job daily, which includes floors, stoves, tabletops, and dishes. Some students are of the opinion that since they are paying high tuition costs they should not have to clean, however I think that cleaning is providing real world lessons in the kitchens in our futures.

Patrice Johnson

MAITRE D'HOTEL BUTTER

1 stick soft unsalted butter
Kosher salt
Italian Parsley - chopped
Lemon zest
Lemon juice
Shallots
Garlic

Mix all ingredients together to form a log. There are no set amounts for
the ingredients, just add the quantity that fits to your own tastes.
Wrap in plastic and freeze. Cut pieces off of the log as needed.
Another neat thing you can do with your butter is to make Veal Kiev.
Here's a Cordon Bleu style veal recipe.

VEAL KIEV

8 oz. veal cutlets
3 oz. Maitre D'Hotel butter (cold)
2 eggs, mixed with ½ cup water
Bread crumbs

Pound pieces of veal between sheets of saran wrap until 1/8" thick.
Season both sides of the veal with salt and pepper.
Fill the inside of the veal with a few pats of the Maitre d'Hotel butter
and fold the veal around the butter as though you were wrapping
a present.
Use A La Anglaise (standard breading procedure) to bread the veal:
Begin by dipping in flour, then eggs & water, and finally, bread
crumbs. Repeat the process with only the eggs and bread crumbs.
This will add a nice thickness to the breading.
Refrigerate for one hour.

Heat oil in sauté pan and brown the veal on all sides. Finish in oven in
the pan.
As it finishes baking, the butter inside will melt and will become the
sauce when the veal is cut open.
This dish can also be made with chicken, turkey or beef. It can be deep
fried, pan fried or baked.
Enjoy!

Uncut - Chapter 15
It is finals week-again!

It may seem hard to believe, because I know it is for me, but it is time for finals again! Where have the last five weeks gone? This time I have decided that I am not going to stress over finals. I've been cooking pretty well for the last several weeks so I am going to pretend that it is just another day at school and cook!

The set up for our finals is different than last time. On the first day we took a written exam for two hours, followed by a test of our knife skills. I am very happy that I took the extra classes offered after school on how to perfect knife cuts. I knew that I wanted a higher grade on my knife cuts this time. The knife cuts are timed and with the exception of the tourné cut, which is seven sided and looks like a miniature football, I was quite successful. My biggest fear during Intro I is gone (picking up the knife), and now the knife cuts seem much easier. I scored over 90% on all of them! Wow, I am making progress. The tourné though, is definitely not one I have mastered and actually never would accomplish it during my time at school (or since).

The final started with everyone receiving a fresh chicken. This, we were to fabricate (cut up) into the required pieces of chicken. We had just completed our knife cuts which we had placed on a sheet tray on the shelf underneath our tables. My partner was the first one to be called up to the chef instructor's desk with his knife cuts. He had already started to cut up his chicken, and without thinking, immediately reached underneath the table to take out his knife cuts. The chef instructor slammed him "Weren't you just touching raw chicken?" Oh no, I thought, what a way to begin the final. My partner looked at me with fear in his eyes and quickly walked over to the hand washing sink to thoroughly wash his hands. I felt confident that he made the right decision and also thankful that he had made the mistake first, since now, I would not repeat it. As he took his tray of knife cuts to the instructor, I watched out of the corner of my eye. The chef instructor was not happy. You will recall that they have a real issue with chicken. He took the tray from him and said "I will be throwing these vegetables away. I don't know what you're going to do about the roulade you were going to need them for." Not to worry, we all took care of him by sparing some of our vegetable cuts. Still, he took a huge cut in his grade as a result of this simple error. It makes an impression on you though. I don't handle chicken to this day without a bleach bottle right next to me!

The next part of our 2-½ day final exam worked like this. The chef instructor passed around a pan filled with small papers listing complete dishes. For each day we drew from the pan one of the papers telling us what we had to make. Each day included one soup, one appetizer, and two complete entrees. We had no recipes to work from and could not talk at all during the finals! Can you imagine? We could not.

I am happy that I kept my cool because my dishes turned out better than I expected. Of course nothing is ever perfect, including my beautiful stuffed potato, which I dropped on the floor when taking it out of the oven. I considered myself lucky since the guy next to me burned his lamb shank so badly that we almost had to bring out the fire extinguishers. He had tears in his eyes and I tried to assure him that the final grade for one dish simply wasn't worth that much of his total grade and that it would be okay. He was ready to bolt from the room and never return, but he hung in there. To this day, I've never been able to think about braising without thinking of his lamb shank. Remember, if you do braise meats, it will most definitely make them more tender. Important to remember though is to check the braising liquid frequently. Under conditions of high heat and also stress (like finals) the braising liquid has a tendency to evaporate quickly! In addition, the ovens aren't always calibrated to the exact temperature that you think. It is for this reason, that my friend and I decide to invest in small oven thermometers. This way, we will always have an accurate measure of the oven temperature. In reality, after purchasing these thermometers we never had time to test the ovens!

Two students decided not to return to take the final, which is worth 50% of our grade. At this point, we have already lost over 30% of our class since we started three short months ago. The kitchen is a lot roomier now and I guess the school must plan for this kind of attrition rate. Now I am beginning to understand why there were so many students on the first day of school.

The chef instructor's have assured us that baking class is much different from the hot foods kitchens and that the pastry chefs are quite snooty. The change to a new class every six weeks is always difficult and much to my surprise I am sorry to leave this one.

After 12 weeks and two introduction classes under my belt, my confidence level is improving. I'm one quarter of the way through the program and I'm doing really well. On the other hand I am totally exhausted. The weekends consist of working on notebooks and studying for tests. In spare time I practice my knife cuts and egg flipping. There is absolutely no time for romantic gourmet picnics with my husband or for entertaining or showing off my cooking skills to friends and family. The trips back and forth each weekend are wearing me out. Studying for the tests seems to be even more intense. Yet one thing remains constant; everyone keeps asking me how much fun I'm having at school and wishing that they could also attend.

Let me take a break to share a favorite recipe with you.

POTATOES DAUPHINOIS

(pronounced Doffin-ah). These are French style au gratin potatoes.

Peel and slice russet potatoes as you would for scalloped potatoes. Dip potatoes in a mixture of heavy whipping cream and milk (equal parts)

Rub a baking dish with butter and sprinkle minced garlic on top of the butter.

Layer the potatoes in the dish with salt and pepper. Top with grated Gruyére cheese and bake at 400 degrees until the cheese is bubbly and brown (about 35-45 minutes).

Variation: Slice and roast red bell peppers. Seed them and puree. Mix in with the potato mixture and follow directions exactly the same as above.

Don't know how to roast red peppers? Culinary 101 here:

If you have a gas stove, place the pepper right on the flame and let the skin get black. Keep turning the pepper until it is black on all sides. Do not attempt to get it white hot; you want the skin black. If you do not have a gas stove, use your grill, it works great.

Place the blackened peppers in a bowl and cover with plastic.

When the peppers are cool use a towel to wipe the black off of them.

You now have roasted peppers.

Wow your friends with this simple and impressive gourmet side dish.

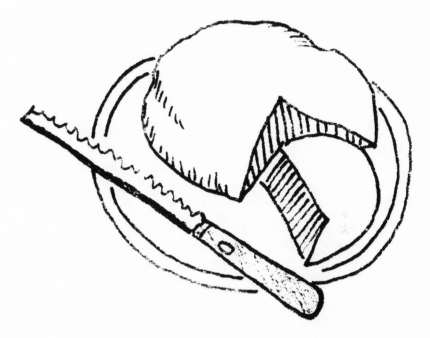

Uncut - Chapter 16
The Breads of Our Labors

It is the moment I've been waiting for since school started, it is my baking class! My only hope going into the class is that it will be a little bit easier than cooking hot foods. I'm also thankful that it will give me a break away from my knives and of course from the flounder!

Baking has always been my favorite since I used to bake bread with my grandmother as a little girl. In those days, we took our bread dough out to the car in the summer where the yeast went wild and nearly flowed over the top of the bowl. The warm kitchens at school seem to be providing the same effect. Being at the baking campus in the summer is quite a concept, since we were told that we cannot have the fans turned on in the kitchens because they disturb the yeast. There isn't room at the new school facility for the baking labs which is another omitted item in the preliminary school tour which I received. Many of us remember our sanitation class where they warned us that we would pass out in the 115 degree kitchens this summer and we are very worried. The new campus of course has air conditioning!

Our immediate concern has been the chef instructors. Were they really as snooty as we heard they were when we left the main campus? In fact, we were pleasantly surprised. Our instructors seemed friendly and happy to have us there. They surprised us by making some great breakfasts and we were also surprised to learn that they also know how to cook not just bake!

Our class continues to get smaller. At this point, we have gone from 36 students to 25. There is much more room to cook, but I'm wondering if this is the typical drop-out rate, and if so, when does it slow down? Our class has developed a real closeness and a great deal of camaraderie. We are always very sad when we lose another one of us.

The chef instructors told us to be sure to make mistakes in class, because that way we can learn. Oh, I knew I was going to like this class! Right from the beginning, I volunteer to be the one who makes mistakes. THIS is right up my alley!

First we learned how to make French bread baguettes that began with a typical chef instructor make-it-look-simple demonstration. The bread is baked in a large steam injection oven. Inside, it looks and moves just like a ferris wheel. We place our bread on proof boards, which are sprinkled with cornmeal, so that they will not stick. Proof boards are actually just thin pieces of plywood cut into large squares. When the ferris wheel stops we place our proof board inside the oven and in one swift motion, tilt the board so that the bread slips off easily and onto one of the shelves that line the wheel. My baguettes look like lightening bolts as they form curves while sliding off of my board. Once they hit the oven shelf, they immediately stick, so there is no way to straighten them out. Great. I told you I was going to like this baking class! I like being the one to make the mistakes, that way the other students don't feel so bad. Seriously, I am enjoying learning about how to knead dough, mix yeast and make bread.

Did you ever hear of starch retrogradation? Well, of course you have, you just didn't know it was called that. Basically it is the staling of bread. Bread begins to get stale as soon as you take it out of the oven, so it is important to freeze bread if you aren't going to eat it right away. By doing this, you help to slow down the staling process. We also learned how to refresh our bread. Simply take it out of the freezer and bake it in a 350 degree oven for 5-10 minutes. This will make the bread seem as though you had just baked it.

SWEET BREAD DOUGH

1 pkg. dry yeast
½ cup warm water
½ teaspoon sugar
½ cup Crisco
1 egg
¼ cup granulated sugar
1 teaspoon salt
2 cups warm water
8 cups bread flour
Dissolve yeast in ¼ cup warm water.
Add egg, remaining water and ix.
Add yeast.
Add flour slowly.
Add salt (Remember salt will kill yeast if added directly to the yeast)

Knead dough for 8-10 minutes, until dough is smooth. Place in a bowl in a warm spot, covered.

First Fermentation: let your dough rise to double in size. Punch it down.

Second fermentation: Let dough rise to double in size. Punch it down, and then form it into loaves.

Proof: this means let the loaves sit in a warm environment until the dough feels full like a marshmallow. Our baking labs had large specialty glass proof boxes with racks to place our proof boards on. Likely you don't have one of these at your house, so just place the dough in a warm spot where there isn't a draft and cover it. Be careful not to let your dough sit too long, or it will be over-proofed. Over proofing also means more carbon dioxide than necessary has been generated. Over proofing can cause the bread to have a sour flavor.

Egg wash and slash. Make your egg wash from one egg, water, and a dash of salt. To use the wash take a small paint brush and paint the wash on your bread. The egg wash will give your bread color and shine. Take a sharp knife and create slashes in the bread. This will allow the expanding gases to release when the bread hits the hot oven.

Patrice Johnson

Bake bread in a hot oven at 450ºF. until golden brown and 200ºF. internal temperature. Take the temperature of your bread at the underside of the loaf using a kitchen thermometer. This will keep you from having a big hole in the top of your bread from the thermometer.

Be sure to cool your bread completely before cutting it or it will be doughy. If you don't plan to use the bread right away, cool and then wrap it and store it in your freezer. To refresh the bread for serving, heat it in a hot oven for five minutes and it will be almost as good as when you first baked it.

Uncut - Chapter 17
Bread Bakers!

At the end of week one, we are becoming experts at bread baking. I never knew there could be this many different kinds of bread! Bread is considered to be the staff of life, we learn from our chef instructor who is a bread baking guru! Up to this point we have all carried our thin knife roll with us daily. For baking though we need a long list of new tools and hardly any of our knives. The chef instructor suggests that we get tool boxes to carry all of our new items in. This is the opportunity that we have been waiting for! The next day all students arrive with new boxes. Mine is fairly small and light weight, but some are large enough to carry an entire line of Craftsman tools. You see, we are not allowed to take food home from school. Up to this point we have eaten what we want to in the labs and then thrown the rest away. Doesn't that seem like such a waste? With all these wonderful breads we are just dying to take them home to our families. With our current workload there is no way that we have time to do any baking at home, so we need these treats. Therefore, at the end of each day we stuff as many as we can into the bottom of our tool boxes. A few times I actually took tools out of my tool box to get more bread and rolls into it. One student pronounced proudly to me every day "This puppy is going home with me tonight," as he removed his bread from the oven.

We learned that ground grain was one of civilized man's first foods. Ancient methods of grinding can be traced to the Far East, Egypt and Rome. As long ago as 6,700 B.C., man ground grains with rocks. Anthropologists believe that man first chewed the raw wheat kernel before he learned to make it into flour and later mix it with water for porridge.

Approximately 3,000 B.C., the ancient Egyptians began to bake white leavened bread similar to the bread we are familiar with today. They fermented the mixture with wild yeast present in the air.

Until the 15th century, bread not only took care of hunger, but it was used as a plate. A thick slice of stale bread was used as a base, which the wealthy used to eat their meats and vegetables. These bases were known as trenchers and were given to dogs or the poor. I thought we had learned all of this in food history. And believe me we were responsible for knowing this stuff on the exams which were held each and every week.

Yeast is a very important component in making bread. A member of the fungi family, it is used as a live bread leavener. Yeast, when fed sugars, expels carbon dioxide and alcohol which is what makes bread rise (and beer brew). It must have moisture, oxygen, sugar and warmth. Remember, yeast dies at 138 degrees, so keep an eye on the temperature of the liquids you add to it. In class, we always mix our yeast with room temperature water. The important thing is not to add salt until after you have added your bread flour. Salt is an enemy of yeast and will kill it if you add it at the beginning of your mixing process.

Salt is an important ingredient in your bread though, because it enhances the flavor, builds structure in the gluten, aids in digestion, and bleaches the bread. When the chef instructors tasted our bread they always knew when we forgot the salt!

Speaking of salt, in school we use only kosher, non-iodized salt. Try the difference in a taste test and I promise you that you won't cook with iodized salt again. Kosher salt is available at the grocery store. You will notice that the grains are larger but the flavor is actually more mild.

When substituting kosher salt in your recipes, you should actually use 50% more salt. Kosher salt won't dissolve completely on your meats and fish. It is kosher salt which I believe is one of the great secrets to flavor in gourmet cooking.

Did you know that flour has to age? Like fine wine, flour must also age! As it ages, it naturally oxidizes, turning a lighter color. Flour that is bleached ages faster. As you might have guessed, unbleached flour is more expensive because it is aged naturally with no chemicals added.

So, is there a difference between bread flour and regular flour? You bet! Make sure you use bread flour to bake bread because it contains the most gluten and the highest amount of protein. The higher in protein the wheat, the better it is for your bread. Gluten is the structure that forms within the dough and give you the ability to trap liquids and gases. Gluten is a protein that is formed when water and wheat flour are mixed. It gives bread dough elasticity and strength.

We're learning to make round dinner rolls this week and boy, the chef instructors sure makes it look simple! I cannot seem to manage this feat no matter how much I try not to twist and turn my wrist. The idea is to form the dough into a ball and then roll it, in a circular motion, very fast on the table so that the dough forms a neat circle on the bottom of the roll. The poor chef instructor, after two days of watching me struggle couldn't stand it anymore! She put her hand over mine and held my wrist straight. Wow! It was so easy! Don't you wish you had a chef instructor in your kitchen every night?

The chef instructors in baking are nothing like what we were told they would be by our previous instructors! We had heard from the last chef instructors about how snooty they are, but it seems much more the opposite! These chef instructors join us every day for the last hour of class and clean with us. This is a first since school started and we are all having trouble getting used to seeing a chef instructor cleaning! They also routinely make us special treats; the latest one being French toast made from our home made French bread. What a treat! For an unusual gourmet twist, the next time you make French toast, try adding a sprinkle of black pepper. You will be surprised by the interesting flavor this brings out when combined with the sweetness of the maple syrup.

Our baking class began by learning how to identify the different types of flour by look and touch. Product identification is extremely popular with the chef instructors. I'm thinking to myself, how often do you go to the store and have to figure out what something is by look and touch? They'd throw you out of the store if you were to try opening bags of flour and touching the product! But it is not my place to question, right? One thing I can tell you for sure, is that we all dread product ID tests which seem to happen at least once a week.

One day the chef instructor told us to bring in four baggies. These we would use to take home the different types of flour so that we could memorize how they looked and felt. I honestly thought that she must be kidding, but she was dead serious. I packaged up the flours and took them home to my apartment where I spent the next week trying to discern the difference. I hope none of my neighbors saw me sitting outside with my hand inside a baggie of white stuff. At the end of the week there they were, all were lined up on the product ID table for test time. Boy, it sure was easier to identify them when I had the marked baggie in front of me! Just for fun they had also thrown in some baking soda, baking powder, and dry milk powder. Every week I tell my friend that I despise product ID tests! These tests are getting harder and the number of items on the product ID section of the test are increasing each week. The latest trick the chef instructors pulled on us was pan spray. None of us guessed it and although it was only worth one point, we all groused for days that this test was completely unfair.

Save yourself the time and trouble of memorizing these. I've already gone through the torture. Don't worry, these flours will always be marked by name at your local store.

AP (all purpose) flour is white flour. It gives the best results for
many kinds of products. It is enriched and can be bleached or
unbleached. It contains 8-11% protein. This is the flour you will
most likely see at the grocery store.

Bread flour is white flour that has been blended with a high protein
wheat giving it greater gluten strength and protein content than
AP flour. It is always unbleached. It typically has a protein content
of 12-14%. Try using it in your chocolate chip cookies for a really
fabulous cookie.

Cake flour is silky and fine in texture. It is used to make cakes, cookies, and some types of pastry. It has the greatest percentage of starch but less protein, which keeps the cakes and pastries delicate. (and just in case you are wondering, yes, it does feel very silky which helped to make it easier to identify although it often fooled us for pastry flour!)

Pastry flour can be used for cookies and cakes. It is finer in texture and lighter in consistency. You frequently will see it added to the top of breads to create a rough texture appearance.

We mastered the ever-popular Foccacia, and I thought you might want to also!

POTATO FOCCACIA

2 oz. cake yeast
9 ½ oz. water
1 potato
¼ oz. kosher salt
Bread flour as needed. (there is not a set amount of bread flour). You will add flour slowly until the bread reaches a dough consistency that is not sticky and that can be kneaded.

Boil or bake potato. If you boil it, the bread will be moister.
Mash the potato.
Mix yeast and water.
Add mashed potato.
Add flour.
Add salt.
Add rest of flour slowly until dough has reached a kneadable consistency.

First fermentation. Cover, place in warm place and let rise to double in size.
Punch down.
Make free form rounds or any shape that you like. Make the shapes somewhat flat.
Second fermentation happens as you work with the dough.

Proof. (This won't take long. Remember, you're looking for your dough
   to be full and resemble a marshmallow).
Coat your fingertips with olive oil. Press your oiled fingertips into the
   freeform round making little indentations. This is called docking.
Add garnish to the top of the bread, over the olive oil. Garnish can
   be sun-dried tomatoes, onions, garlic, herbs or anything else you
   want to add.

Brush garnish with olive oil so that it doesn't burn.
Bake in a 450°F oven until golden brown.
Cool before slicing.

Uncut - Chapter 18
The Finality of Baking

Baking I has ended and it's time for finals. The format is different than finals from our previous classes and will span several days. Probably the biggest difference is that after we finish the written portion and draw our menus, then we will be allowed to use our notebooks to write down the recipes on a total of five recipe cards. Remember cheat sheets? Of course, writing the recipes down is the easy part! Making the breads and sweets look the way they are supposed to look is a completely different story.

I had decided earlier that if I drew too tough of a menu I would just forego the remainder of finals. Fortunately, I am fairly pleased with my picks and decide to stick it out. There were a few items that I absolutely did not want to make again. Swans were one of them. Why? Because my fellow students are still howling with laughter at the thought of my first attempt at Swans. Guess what? Now I had to make a half dozen! I was also expected to make six Danish pinwheels, an 8" chocolate raspberry tart, two types of bread, a quart of Italian Meringue, and demonstrate my knife cuts on apples. I had the remainder of that day, the next day and the weekend to ponder my menu and do what I could complete in class before the final presentation on Monday. It was up to me come up with my own production schedules of how I should plan my time.

Danish falls into the category of a "laminated dough". Laminated dough that you are probably familiar with are Danish pastries, croissants, and puff pastry. On the day we made laminated dough in class there was a great deal of frustration among the students. Laminated dough contains many layers of butter, which is what makes them so flaky. A great deal of butter is incorporated into the dough and you must roll it in and turn the dough through several series of turns to fully incorporate all of the butter. It is not easy to do this and the dough must rest in between turns, which makes it very time consuming. You must be very careful not to roll your rolling pin off the edge of the dough as this will create a hole in the dough and when you bake it, the melted butter will leak out of your product and into your pan. The result will be that your Danish will look flatter and not poofy. They won't be as flaky either.

Danish pastry came into being when the Danish bakers went on strike in the late 19th century. They were replaced by Viennese bakers who produced a light, flaky, pastry dough. When the Danish bakers returned to work, they adopted the Vienna way of preparing dough, added some variations and fillings, and took credit for it, thus the name Danish. Now, we all know who to blame for the fact that we are having to make these little lovelies for our final!

You've likely seen Danish in many varieties. For my final, I was making pinwheels filled with blackberry jam. I wasn't concerned about making Danish; I felt super confident. Danish and laminated dough, I had mastered! We all took our places at our assigned tables after writing down our recipes. Once we wrote them down, we were not allowed to look at our notebooks again and of course there was to be no talking. I found my spot, set up my tools and walked in the walk in refrigerator. It felt extremely cold today. I grabbed a package of yeast and some eggs. I had trouble finding an egg that wasn't broken. I opened up the package of yeast and it had ice crystals on it. Our chef instructor had informed us during the class that yeast can be frozen, so I wasn't too concerned about it. Soon I realized that the eggs were frozen. No way! I thought. Would they really do this to us on purpose? Those little devils. They had given us product which was bad to make the final more challenging.

I sighed, thinking of the complications this was going to cause as I picked up a frozen milk bottle. Just then the chef instructor came in and told us that there had been a problem with the walk in last night. They were bringing us new products to use. Whew, I thought, what a relief. I actually have a chance here, except for the swans of course.

Making the Danish dough was easier than I remembered from the first time and they turned out pretty darn good! I did however nearly burn the blackberry jam on the stove. Fortunately one of the other students gave me a look (because we aren't allowed to talk). I clued in to go over to the stove where my blackberry jam was nearly boiling over. I tasted it when it cooled down a bit and didn't taste any burned flavor, so I considered it a save, thankful that I wouldn't have to redo it. There simply wasn't time to make things more than once in finals.

On the last day of our final exam, by lunchtime, all products had to be displayed on our table with a printed menu included. This had been a difficult final since it had been going on for four days now. While we took a rare lunch break, the chef instructors graded our various products. We all thought seriously about going out for drinks to calm our nerves, but the chef instructors had warned us that if we came back drunk we would fail the entire class. It wasn't worth the risk, so we stuck with iced tea. When we returned from our break, they had not finished their grading. I noticed that my swans looked warm and tired after setting out in the kitchen for two hours. I hoped the chef instructors had seen them earlier when they were fresher, although even when first presented, they didn't resemble swans, looking more like eagles or vultures. The chef instructors spotted us looking in through the windows and shooed us away. They said they needed more time. Of course, we couldn't help ourselves and continued our peeking, trying to see what they thought of our final products. Soon we were shocked to witness a lemon meringue tart flying through the kitchen and hitting the very window we were peering through. We all held our breath because we had never seen the chef instructors do anything like this! We must have made them very angry! But then they started laughing and we all ran back into the room and placed our beautiful final products right into the trash.

My goodness, is it really possible that another six weeks have ended? I remember the instructors telling us on the first day that they don't give out A's in Baking I, but I am hopeful nonetheless. During the exit interview I find out that in fact I have aced the finals and the class, but not the swans!

Patrice Johnson

PUMPERNICKEL BREAD

4 ½ oz. sourdough starter
2 oz. water
1 oz. plain yogurt
¾ oz. cake yeast
2 oz. coffee, brewed
2 oz. molasses
2 tablespoons lekvar
1 ½ oz. butter, room temperature
¾ teaspoon cocoa powder
1 ½ teaspoon caraway seeds, toasted and ground fine
¼ oz. Salt
3 oz. Pumpernickel flour
Bread flour as needed to thicken dough

Combine ingredients beginning with liquid.
Add yeast, sourdough starter, water, yogurt, coffee (cooled), molasses, lekvar and butter.
Add pumpernickel flour and cocoa powder.
Next add slat and toasted caraway seeds.
Add bread flour.

Knead dough for 6-8 minutes.
Keep covered and let rise until doubled in size.
Punch down.
Shape into a large round loaf.
Place loaf on a sheet pan which has been sprayed, lined with parchment paper and sprayed again.
Proof – let the bread rest, covered until it has the consistency of a marshmallow.

Wash with a mixture of water and molasses.
Slash the bread three times across the top with a very sharp knife.
Bake in 350 degree oven until golden brown and internal temperature of 200 degrees.

SOURDOUGH STARTER

2 oz. yeast
24 oz. water
Bread flour

Make starter and let ferment (covered) for at least 7 days.

Mix yeast with water and add enough bread flour to make a pancake like consistency.

Place starter in a draft free place. Don't let it be subjected to direct heat or high temperatures. If your starter has been sitting for a long time it may develop a gray liquid on top of the batter. This can be mixed back into the starter.

Don't forget to replenish the starter each time you use it. Measure the amount required for your recipe and replace equal parts flour and liquid to the sourdough starter container.

What is lekvar? Lekvar is a thick fruit spread made from prunes or apricots and then cooked with sugar. It is a Hungarian specialty often used in making cookies and pastries. You should be able to find it at your grocery store.

Patrice Johnson

Uncut - Chapter 19
Celebrating the Move to Baking II

It is our first day in Baking II and we all have lots of confidence after Baking I; we are feeling good, we're ready to go! We met our new chef instructors and they began demonstrating how to make triple layer cakes. That doesn't look too bad we think, however, panic started to set in when they began decorating the cakes!

The student next to me showed me his notebook where he was trying to diligently sketch these complicated decorated cakes. I didn't even attempt to draw them, which was my first clue that I wasn't going to have much fun making them. I noted that across the top of the page he had scrawled, "There's just no way." I couldn't agree more. Not long after that, he left for the remainder of the day, and I couldn't blame him one bit!

The kitchen temperature is normally upward of 90 degrees and I'm starting to feel giddy. Lucky for us the ovens aren't even turned on. The giddiness is starting to get worse. This could be from the heat, but I think it is from the sight of these cakes. One is called a buffet cake, and the other is a celebration cake. We haven't even had a one day break since Baking I ended just yesterday, so I'm hardly in the mood for celebration cakes of any kind! The chef instructor recommends that we purchase a set of decorating tips (25 in all), and I'm thinking, "I really think plain white cakes are pretty and elegant, don't you?" But let me tell you, after three days in this class, the first day looked comparatively easy. In fact, those cakes were a picnic compared to what was yet to come. We're in the advanced baking class now my friend kept reminding me. This made me think that I needed to get back to those relaxing bread baking days we had in Baking I.

I started working on my celebration cakes and they were a disaster right from the beginning. For one thing, my sponge cakes were about 1" high and the chef instructor seemed to think that I could divide each of them into three layers. I told her that was definitely in the impossible area, and even she, seeing the height of my cakes, had to agree. We settled on double layers. Next, it was time to start icing the suckers using buttercream. Have you ever made buttercream? Trust me, you don't want to go there. Take it from one who really has had the experience. I recommend that you just get those little cans of icing already made at the store. This buttercream is at the flounder level. It is very temperamental, and if it gets too cold you have to use a blow torch to warm the mixing bowl up. If it gets too hot, you have to put the bowl in an ice bath. I don't know about you, but prior to culinary school I wasn't keeping a blow torch in my kitchen on a regular basis. In any event, my butter cream is too cold, and then of course I get it too hot. I play around with that buttercream as long as possible, primarily to avoid having to start working on the celebration cake.

Before I started Baking I was convinced that I wanted to be a pastry chef! I think I do have potential for creating Halloween goodies since the writing on my celebration cakes was rather shaky, crooked, and downright spooky. Other than that, let's face it, my skills as a pastry chef are over! The buffet cake was even worse. On the top of the buffet cake we were to divide it into 20 pieces just marking them lightly with a knife across the top of the icing on the cake. On the inner circle we were to divide it into 4 pieces; thus allowing for a total of 24 slices pre-marked for the ease of cutting. I can't even draw a straight line with a ruler, so this, for me, was quite an impossible task! Just when I thought it couldn't get any better the chef instructor came over to help me learn how to make roses. I could not and can not make roses. My friend stood next to me and made 24 perfect roses. She tried to show me how, two chef instructors tried to instruct me how, but I could not do it. These roses were to look identical; one for each of the 24 slices of cake. The butter cream looked awful. It was streaky and melted and pieces of cake were showing through it. The roses didn't help to improve the situation, nor did the fact that the chef instructor seemed to think each rosebud should have a stem. This, I considered to be one of my worst days to date at school. It was way beyond the flounder. I couldn't wait to leave for the day.

Lots of people have asked me what I want to do when I finish school. My response from the beginning has been that I need to see where I excel and what I enjoy the most. Cake decorating, I've decided, is not my forte! In fact, at this point in culinary school I'm thinking I don't really excel in anything at all!

I do enjoy baking cakes, as long as I don't have to decorate them. The next day we made a great devil's food cake! Devil's food is dark, dense, rich and moist. It dates back to the early 1900's. It received its name because it is so rich and delicious that it must be sinful. The cake is named for its dark red brown color, which comes from the baking soda that neutralizes the acid of the chocolate and leavens the cake. See how the chemistry lessons just go on and on? For our purposes we made our devil's food into a yummy, Black Forest Cake, three layers high, and decorated to the hilt with cherries and whipped cream. When I see the finished product (which contains no roses or writing, yeah!) I decide that maybe a career as a pastry chef isn't totally out of the question. Of course I draw this conclusion late one night over homework and my second or third glass of wine!

Funny story about the Black Forest Cakes. To store them for the evening we placed each one on a sheet tray which then was placed on a tall speed rack which is a metal rack that can hold several rows of sheet trays. In order to protect the cakes from the walk in refrigerator, we would

Patrice Johnson

"cater wrap" the entire rack. This was done by starting at the top with a large roll of plastic wrap. As one student held the wrap, others would turn the rack quickly and soon the entire rack would be covered with saran wrap. We were rather new to this technique and on this particular day the rack got spinning a little bit too quickly. Unfortunately, this caused my friend's almost finished black forest cake to fly right off of the rack. She was in tears since the chef instructor had not yet graded her on it, and at this point she wouldn't have a chance to make another one. After that day, we never spun the speed racks quite that quickly!

DEVIL'S FOOD CAKE

Yield: two 10" cakes

13 ½ oz. cake flour
1 cup cocoa powder
1 ½ Tablespoon baking soda
½ teaspoon salt
1 pound sugar
3 eggs
10 fl. oz. vegetable oil
12 fl. oz. buttermilk
12 fl. oz. coffee (brewed)

Sift and combine together cake flour, cocoa powder, baking soda and
    salt. Combine vegetable oil, coffee and buttermilk
Whip sugar and egg mixture until full in volume. . Once eggs are at full
    volume, alternately add the dry ingredients to the wet ingredients.
Pour batter into two 10"round pans which have been sprayed with pan
    spray, lined with parchment paper and sprayed again.
Bake in 350 degree oven until firm to the touch in the center,
    approximately 45 minutes.
When a toothpick comes out clean, cake is done.
Let cake cool in pan.
When cool, invert cake onto 10" round cake circle.

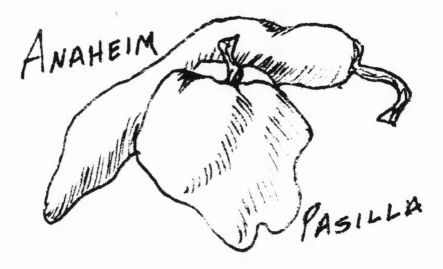

Uncut - Chapter 20
Putting the "H" in HOT!

One thing which was a regular occurrence at school was saying "I have a knife, or knife behind you." This we learned in our early days as part of our safety classes so that we would not accidentally stab someone. Apparently, this has happened at culinary school in the past.

When we started carrying hot pans around the room, we began to routinely say "Hot, behind you." This was quickly shortened to "Hot behind" which was usually followed by something like "Thanks for noticing, I've been working on it." Our class had a wonderful sense of humor and in retrospect; I think that is the only thing that got us all through the school year.

Our class also had a fondness for hot and spicy food. Prior to school, my definition of hot food was a taco from Del Taco with a few drops of mild sauce. At school, the students loved to cook and did so every chance they got. By the time we arrived to Baking II, the new chef instructors were quite unprepared for our group. Every morning students walked boldly into the walk in refrigerator, grabbed some eggs brought them out to a table and mixed them up into a wonderful omelet for all of us to share. This had become quite a routine for several months now, but the chef instructors in Baking II were not going for it. They told us we had to ask for food, particularly eggs, of which there may not be enough. This really put a damper on the whole thing, so we just started bringing in our own food to cook. Eating together was part of our camaraderie. We longed for real food after all of these long weeks in baking.

We had learned early on at school that eating and drinking was generally okay in the classrooms, however the school frowned upon having fast food in the building. I guess they didn't think that would provide the right image for folks who were gazing in the windows at the students. I've never been much of a fast food person, but I seemed to crave burgers more than ever while at school.

One day while carrying a hot pan across the room, I shouted out "H-O-T pan". Everyone burst out laughing. I accentuated the "t" to make it sound like "TAY" and H-O-T became an every day saying in our class. The chef instructors had no idea why we started spelling hot, but it stuck for the rest of our school days and as time went by, we thought it was even funnier.

It was well known that I didn't like hot food, so other students were always quick to give me something spicy to taste. Invariably, the food was always extremely hot. Their favorite ingredient was Habanero chilies, so I always got a really hot mouthful!

We made all of our ice cream for use in our Baking II class. The school was planning an ice cream contest, so naturally our class decided on Habanero crisp ice cream. They made a Habanero type peanut brittle and mixed it into the ice cream. The cold-hot sensation was something else, and I'm sure you can appreciate that we didn't win the contest.

Speaking of H-O-T, have you ever made caramel? Although we had all been burned here and there in the kitchen, the serious burns began when we learned to make caramel. Making caramel was not easy to say the least. Was anything in baking easy?? The chef instructor warned us to be sure to have a container of ice water nearby for our burns. Sugar caramelizes at 338 degrees, so basically when the caramel touches your skin it is definitely H-O-T! This perpetuated many more instances of our use of the word 'hot' and also some fun pot washing! Getting caramel out of the bottom of the pots was next to rocket science. Caramel in theory is relatively easy to make. You take some granulated sugar and mix it with water using your hand so that you can determine it to be the texture of wet sand. Once you have achieved this wet sand concept, you put the pot on the stove on the highest possible heat. Using your paintbrush you dip it into ice water and wash down the inside of the pot. This is to prevent the caramel from crystallizing. Because, as we all quickly learn, once caramel crystallizes, you are done. What I mean by done, is that you will be starting over. This is a total pain in the neck. Because the pot is now a sticky mess and it is not easy to get out the sugar which is stuck to the bottom of the pot. In order to do this, you must fill the pot with water and boil it out. I've been making caramel since science projects in grade school, but I could not make it at Cordon Bleu! It crystallized every time, and I pretty much convinced myself that this was because of that which was supposed to prevent the crystallization: ice water! In reality, the sugar had probably been tainted with flour or some other contaminant and once the chef instructor offered us a new bag of sugar, our caramel started to work out better, to a point. Once the sugar begins to turn to caramel, it does so very quickly. This leaves very little time for you to take the pot off of the stove and place it into an ice bath. This will stop the cooking and hopefully you will get it stopped before it is burnt to a crisp. Sometimes, it is down right black, so you know it is burned, but other times it has gone just a second or two longer than it should have and so it has a burnt flavor to it. I decided that I hated making caramel and hoped we'd never see it again. We saw so much caramel in the next several weeks that I absolutely could not comprehend it.

We took the caramel and spun it. If you haven't done this, you should try it, just for the sight of it. The caramel we took out of the pot while it was very h-o-t and using forks tossed it away from us over two dowels hanging off of the table. It formed a very thin angel hair appearance. Then, we balled up the angel hair and put it on top of our dessert. It was absolutely gorgeous for about 20 seconds and then the heat of the kitchen began to take its toll and it would begin to melt. My personal favorite though was taking the caramel and placing it over the back of large pan sprayed ladle to form a caramel cage. When removing it from the ladle you had to be extra careful that it would not break (and it always would). It was definitely another nightmare.

We made caramel decorations shaped like spirals to place in our desserts for added affect. We skewered nuts and dipped them one by one into caramel. We piped caramel out of parchment paper coronets (which absolutely burned our hands every time even through two pairs of gloves). The ultimate caramel experience came near the end of the baking classes. I believe this was deliberate because the instructors probably figured that we had reached our limit at that point. Croquembouche is a French anniversary cake. What is it you ask? It is a tree which is made using cream puffs which are stuck together to form the tree using, you guessed it, caramel! After you stick the puffs together to form the tree (and it takes about a hundred of the suckers plus unlimited number of pots of caramel), you finish the croquembouche with angel hair made from caramel.

CARAMEL SAUCE

2 oz. water
8 ½ oz. granulated sugar
8 oz. heavy cream
2 ½ oz. unsalted butter

Mix water and sugar together using your hand until it feels like wet sand.
Place on medium high heat and cook until mixture achieves a dark caramel color.
Heat cream and butter in separate pan.
Slowly temper cream/butter mixture into the caramel.
Be careful since the caramel is very hot at this point. It will bubble up quickly when you add the cream mixture.

This sauce may be reheated over low heat and served over ice cream or brownies.

Uncut - Chapter 21
Soufflé Secrets

According to our baking book, a great baker must be attentive to technique, details and timing. Unable to taste the food and correct it along the way, the baker must be a stickler for measurements.

I never thought about it like this. But in fact, this is what makes baking so much different; the tasting comes only after the product has been completed. Now at least I have an excuse for why everything is so difficult.

This week we are making soufflés. Soufflé means 'puffed up' and of course that is what we are hoping ours will do!

We are working in new teams this week because the instructors believe that we are all too close to each other and that we should learn to work outside of our comfort zone. This they tell us, will better prepare us for the real world. What the instructors failed to realize was that we all get along superbly and most of us are nonplussed by the fact that we have to work with a new partner this week. My new partner is feeling unsure about his soufflés puffing up. No problem, I tell him, I've made these tons of times (okay once—) at home. Piece of cake… no pun intended.

The team at the table in front of us was most impressed when our soufflés came out of the oven! The soufflés had risen quite tall and looked really fantastic. I hated to break the news to them that having just seen theirs in the oven, they had better go take a look. "What? The one student asked, racing towards the oven with panic in his eyes. What do you mean? I must tell you that this particular student was not at all happy with his new partner for the week. He had been working with the same partner for five consecutive months and he had been pretty convinced from the beginning of the soufflé project that his new partner was going to screw it up. He rushed to the ovens only to see that their soufflés looked exactly like pancakes! Needless to say that he was beyond upset with their fallen soufflés and had to make them again. He looked at me with a grin and took a swig of the Grand Marnier Crème Anglaise. After all, he sure didn't need it for his soufflé any time soon. Drinking as you probably have surmised, was definitely out of the question at school. We were used to seeing lots of wine and brandy in the hot foods kitchen but had been warned early on that they better not catch us drinking it. Most of the wine we used was cheap boxed wine, so we were never really tempted. Once we got to baking they had all the really good liqueurs. These were kept in a locked cage until the time that we needed to use them. This student casually ambled up to the instructor and explained that he needed some Grand Marnier. She never gave it a second thought as she handed him the bottle. Upon returning to his station, he added a few more shots to the crème Anglaise and continued to drink. He was definitely going to be okay now with his new baking partner.

Although they had to repeat the recipe for the soufflé (and possibly for the crème anglaise given how much had been consumed), he had the last laugh, because when we served our soufflés to the instructor they were not fully cooked inside. Remember what I said about how you can't taste your products! And, keep in mind how fantastic they looked!

Now if we had some extras on hand we could have had a small taste. However, the recipe we were given made only two, both of which we were required to present to the chef instructor. We put them back in the oven, they cooked through and still maintained their "poof!

How fast do they fall when taken out of the oven? Immediately! Therefore, it is critical to serve them right away.

What are the tricks to making a soufflé? Preparing a soufflé requires quick and precise steps. Timing is essential. If your nerves are rattled you may find that some Grand Marnier crème anglaise does the trick.

Soufflés can be hot or cold. They can be desserts or savory (not sweet). Baked soufflés are more fragile than cold or frozen ones. This is because there is hot air trapped in the soufflé which begins to escape and this causes the mixture to deflate. This happens as soon as the dish is taken out of the oven.

A soufflé has two components: Stiffly beaten egg whites and a thick, well-seasoned or flavored base. Soufflés are usually baked in a soufflé dish which is round and has straight sides which facilitate the soufflé's rising. Soufflé's are famous for rising to almost double their size. The air which is whipped into the egg whites expands in the oven and makes the soufflé rise.

Frozen soufflés are known as semi-freddo's in Italian and soufflé glace in French. Components of a frozen soufflé are fruit puree, gelatin, Italian meringue and whipped cream.

FROZEN SOUFFLÉ
Serves 8

Cut out eight 14x6" strips of foil. Fold each strip lengthwise in half. Wrap one around each of eight soufflé dishes. Secure with tape if needed.

8 fl. oz. fruit puree (make puree by blending or processing 12 oz. frozen fruits and straining them to get puree)
4 gelatin sheets
5 egg whites
2 cups granulated sugar
water, cold (to bloom gelatin)
16 fl. oz cream

Patrice Johnson

Dissolve gelatin sheets in cold water. Squeeze out excess water.
Heat fruit puree and add gelatin to puree to dissolve.

Make an Italian Meringue using 5 egg whites and 10 oz. Sugar.
Mix sugar and water to a sand like consistency.
Cook over medium heat until the mixture reaches softball stage (115 degrees).

While mixture is cooking whip egg whites in stand mixer.
Be sure that there is no liquid on the bottom of the bowl as the egg whites whip up.
When sugar mixture reaches the softball stage, add it slowly to the bowl of egg whites (while they are still whipping).
After all of the sugar has been added, increase mixer speed.
Whites should have a stiff peak and should still be warm.
Fold Italian Meringue into warm, gelatin mixture.
Whip the cream to medium peaks. Fold cream into puree/meringue mixture.
Pipe mixture from a pastry bag using a plain tip into collared ramekins.
Using a spatula, smooth out the top surface.
Freeze until firm. (overnight is best).
Remove foil collars before serving

Note on gelatin: Sheet gelatin is more expensive than powdered. It is easier to measure for recipes. It must be softened in any amount of cold water. This is known as blooming. Excess water should be squeezed out of the sheet before using it.
Sheet gelatin is available at baking supply stores.

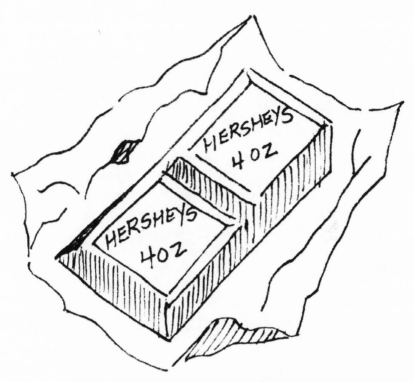

Uncut - Chapter 22
It's Flambé day at Cordon Bleu!

Today we are going to make lots of flambéed desserts! These desserts are known as classic restaurant desserts. I'm still a bit nervous when there is fire around, especially one that we set deliberately! I remember with a bit of anxious thoughts the first time we flambéed in Intro II and how scared I was!

The instructors turn off the lights to demonstrate these impressive dessert techniques. They begged us to please cook the alcohol out of our desserts today so that they won't be too drunk after tasting 100 of them! When flambéing in the professional kitchen, it is necessary to yell out, "Flambé" so that those around you can be warned. We are all learning to say it with a fancy accent to make us feel very French! Of course, we immediately follow our 'Flambé' with an 'H-O-T' and the chef instructors just shake their heads.

Patrice Johnson

We learned how to make Bananas Foster, Cherries Jubilee, Baked Alaska and Crepes Suzette. Cherries Jubilee was created at Café du Paris in Monte Carlo on the French Riviera. Chef Henri Charpentier accidentally made this specialty when he dropped his cordial (which he was drinking) into the pan and it caught fire. As the chef instructor tells the story, the Grand Marnier student gives me a big wink. "Today is going to be extra fun!" he says.

Bananas Foster was created at Brennans restaurant in New Orleans. It was named for Richard Foster who was a frequent patron at the restaurant. It is not difficult to make and will impress your guests. If you buy your ice cream rather than making it like we did, you will save even more time. If you do make it yourself, it is going to taste so much better and making ice cream is relatively easy in the scheme of other things we've tried to master.

LETS GO BANANAS CORDON BLEU STYLE!

2 oz. unsalted butter
½ cup brown sugar, packed
4-5 fl. oz. orange juice (or the juice of one orange)
2-3 oz. dark rum or 2 teaspoons rum extract
1 tsp. pure vanilla extract
2 oz. Grand Marnier
1 banana cut into ½" slices
pinch ground cinnamon
1 large scoop of premium vanilla ice cream.

Melt butter and brown sugar in large pan.
Bring to boil.
Add juice and reduce (lessen the amount of liquid and allow it to become thicker).
Add extract and rum.
Add bananas only to coat them. Don't keep them in the liquid for an extended time or they will become soggy.

Flambé with Grand Marnier. If you add a pinch of cinnamon, it will add spark to your flames!
Serve over a scoop of ice cream.

Note: If you have an electric range it is not as easy to flambé since you
don't have an open flame. You may however, flambé with the use
of your lighter. Pour your liquor into the pan, ignite directly with a
long lighter.

If you are cooking on a gas range, tilt your pan and the liquid will catch
fire from the flame of your stove.

Oh, don't forget to announce FLAMBE!

Patrice Johnson

Uncut - Chapter 23
Chocolate and More Chocolate!

The word chocolate comes from the Aztec word 'xocolatl" which means bitter water. The Aztecs used cocoa beans and spices to make an unsweetened chocolate drink. They believed that chocolate was an aphrodisiac. Most of the world's cocoa plantations are located in West Africa and in Central and South America. Cocoa trees are also grown in some islands of the West Indies, Sri-lanka and the Philippines. The leading cocoa producing countries are Ghana, Brazil, Nigeria, the Ivory Coast, the Cameroon's and Ecuador. Every year we in the U.S. consume more than one third of all of the cocoa produced! The cocoa tree is an evergreen that blooms with tiny white, pink, yellow or red flowers all year round. The cocoa beans are found inside pods which grow directly on the tree trunk. When ripe, the pods look like red, orange or golden footballs. The beans are fermented and dried, then go through an elaborate production process before becoming chocolate. Each tree produces about a thousand pods, however only 200 make it to full term. When the beans arrive at the chocolate factory they are roasted at 250-350 degrees for one hour. They do not smell like chocolate until after they are roasted. The factor that determines the flavor of the chocolate is how long the beans are actually roasted. After roasting, the beans are removed from their pods, fermented, dried, roasted and cracked. The cocoa beans are blended together and the nibs are ground into an extract. The liquid that remains is the chocolate liquor. This liquor is refined. If the cocoa butter is extracted from the liquor, the remainder is ground to make cocoa power. If no sugar, flavoring, or cocoa butter is added to the chocolate liquor, it is bitter and what is known as unsweetened chocolate or baker's chocolate. If other things are added, for example, milk powder and sugar, it becomes what we know and love; milk chocolate.

How do I know all of these interesting chocolate facts? Because we sat in a three hour lecture one morning to learn them. Aren't you grateful for the abbreviated format?

In class we used more chocolate than I've ever seen! At the end of the day our aprons and towels were chocolate coated and believe it or not, we did get tired of eating it! Our class was well known for having a sweet tooth, but let's face it, after 12 weeks of baking even we are tired of all sweets! It definitely took additional effort to get the chocolate stains out of the aprons and chef jackets. Every morning we compare notes on what products work best to remove the stains of chocolate. We've tried all of the products on the market. Our chef whites were beginning to take on an ugly grey hue; one that we never totally lost after Baking II. It was almost as though a reminder to us of our baking days and how we could never forget them. To this day, I think of those days in baking class whenever I have to bake something, and I long for the days when I was young and baking was my passion.

Have you ever noticed that chocolate you put in the refrigerator gets little beads of perspiration on it? This is called sugar bloom and it occurs when a layer of sugar syrup (white stuff) is released when exposed to moisture. Now, if you've ever left a candy bar to melt in your car and then looked at it after it had regained its solid state you would see white on the chocolate. This is called fat bloom that is released due to exposure to the heat. There isn't anything wrong with chocolate that has fat or sugar bloom so don't worry about eating it. The only negative is that it doesn't look attractive and as you know at Cordon Bleu, presentation is everything! They taught us how to take the temperature of chocolate and melt it perfectly so we wouldn't have these problems. Now let's face it, you and I have been dipping strawberries in chocolate for years without taking the temperature and they were wonderful! Chocolate, it seems, is much more temperamental than we ever knew!

Making chocolate truffles bordered on rocket science for me. Once I started tempering chocolate (melting a portion of the chocolate, measuring the temperature and then carefully mixing in another portion of chocolate), my truffles weren't setting up and I was getting frustrated. Why can't we just melt chocolate in the microwave like we do at home and dip the suckers? Trust me, it works out really well. I've been doing it successfully for years, and now I can't make a darn truffle to save my life. But if I could make one, the chocolate would look beautiful; no fat or sugar bloom!

Naturally, my truffles were special; full of sugar and fat bloom and dipping them into the deep recesses of chocolate (and finding them again, proved to be quite a trick!). None the less, they tasted wonderful. I took them home to the family and everyone was duly impressed. I was sure to tell everyone how much fun I had making them and what a breeze it was.

For you at home, just melt chocolate the way you've always done. Dip your berries and truffles and you'll be so much happier. Do not buy a chocolate thermometer, and do not try to temper chocolate. Why? Because it is not FUN!

Rather than dip chocolates at all, instead, try this recipe.

TOOTSIE ROLLS

1 lb. dark chocolate (melted)
4 ½ fl. oz. light corn syrup

Melt chocolate and corn syrup over a bain marie. Bain marie is a hot water bath underneath your bowl. Never melt chocolate directly on the heat of the stove.
Roll mixture out with a rolling pin between two sheets of plastic wrap.
Refrigerate until it is set up.
Remove from refrigerator and knead to soften.

Patrice Johnson

Form into any shape you want and wrap in wax paper. You can really
    get creative and cut shapes out with cutters.
The kids will love them!

CHOCOLATE MOUSSE
Serves 2

5 oz.	heavy cream, whipped
2 oz.	butter, unsalted
5.5 oz.	dark chocolate
2	egg yolks
1.5 oz.	sugar
¼ oz.	brandy
2	egg whites

Melt chocolate, butter and brandy over bain marie
Whip egg yolks with ½ sugar to ribbon stage.
Whip whites and ½ sugar to medium peaks.
Fold eggs into chocolate.
Fold in whipped cream.
Put in ramekins and chill.

HERSHEY BAR FROSTING (From my grandmother)

½ lb.butter
6 Hershey chocolate bars
2 egg yolks
6 tablespoons powdered sugar

Melt candy bars.
Using a mixer beat egg yolks and butter until light yellow.
Add powdered sugar and mix well.
Slowly pour in melted chocolate. Beat until smooth.

Wonderful on your favorite cake!

Uncut - Chapter 24
The End of 12 LONG Weeks

Well, it sure is fun having a final every six weeks. Let me tell you, they come around fast! I'm still remembering those eagle swans I made for my Baking I final when I learn the really good news about the Baking II final. This will be a test of ALL of our baking talents. All 12 weeks worth! The chef instructor is telling us this and I'm actually laughing out loud. Now, the chef instructor wants to know what I'm laughing at. Recalling how my Baking I items looked, I think, if she could see the pictures of my "swans" she would be crying, not laughing! I try to explain to her that she is hearing my hysterical laugh.

We are literally at the half way point of being done with school now, but who has time to think about that? It is time for another beautiful final and I'm trying to get geared up.

I learned that for this final I have a choice of making a wedding cake, croquembouche or some type of sugar art. Well, those are about the three worst choices I can think of. I decide on the lesser of all evils, but still a complete nightmare; the wedding cake!

Patrice Johnson

We have already had the pleasure of making a wedding cake once this term. This fun little project was mandatory and if I didn't drop out of school after it, I probably am not going to. The good news about the wedding cake was that we didn't have to actually bake a cake. Little did I know, that baking the cake would have been the easy part. Instead, my friend and I headed down to the local craft store where we purchased Styrofoam rounds to use for the "cake". In school the next day we learned how to take fondant and roll it out and place it on the rounds. Fondant is pretty cool stuff. It actually comes in a large bucket and you just take what you need, roll it out in powdered sugar and place it on your cake. It provides for a very smooth surface and looks really elegant. The kicker is that you basically have one shot to get it on the cake. Fondant, I learned, is not like wall plaster, which you can go over and over several times. It is a ONE TIME deal to make it fit on the cake and all be rolled the same thickness. Let's face it, you know about gravity and so I put the fondant on the cake layer and it starts breaking off (not where I want it to, of course). This looks lovely, as I'm sure you can imagine. If you have ever seen a cracked plaster wall, then you get the idea. The chef instructor in her infinite wisdom tells me not to worry. The decorators icing will cover up any problems with the fondant. Decorators icing? Oh yes, she demonstrates on her cake. You just start piping out your decorations on to the wedding cake and the fondant is covered up. Decorations??? I thought I had already established that I like plain white cakes. Now, I'm going to decorate a wedding cake? To say that day was a nightmare would be a grave understatement. Therefore, it is not a happy moment when I learn that I will get to repeat the experience.

In addition to the wedding cake, I must make a dozen raspberry linzer tartlets. Thinking back to making one linzer tartlet in Baking I, I conclude that I am going to fail this final. Linzer dough is very hard to work with. In fact, if you look at it or attempt to touch it, it basically falls apart in your hands. That, in of itself, wouldn't be too bad, but to form a dozen of them into tiny 3" tart pans and then cut small thin strips and criss cross them over each other, is virtually the next closest thing to putting one up into space.

I also have to make a dozen chocolate truffles and making them with temperatures of near 95 in the classroom is going to be a challenge to say the least. The fact that I have to temper the chocolate rather than using my microwave is absolutely going to hurt me. Next on the list is a Dobos Torte. Again, rocket science. Eight layers of cake filled with chocolate butter cream and topped with six caramel wedges. Another fun one for sure, but one that I had mastered fairly well the first time through. Probably beginners luck. The good news: no writing required on the cake! It could have been worse. Some lucky people had to make celebration cakes. I counted my blessings. The only good news that I get is the 12 mini Danish. Those, I can handle! I'm the only one in the class that enjoyed making the Danish. Laminated dough is a treat that everyone should enjoy. Many people almost dropped out of baking I during the week of laminated dough, but I actually thought it was fun.

I have 2 ½ days to complete all of these final items and that seemed like a long time. I'm extremely relieved to learn that there is no writing necessary on the wedding cake, but then I learn that we have to submit two cake rounds with a sample of piped writing on them. I asked the instructor in all seriousness if my entire presentation could be a Halloween theme? She did not seem to find this amusing. How am I going to get through this baking final?

I made the wedding cake first to get it out of the way. It was actually just as hard as the first time and the fondant had huge cracks in it that I couldn't seem to smooth out (without wall plaster). I asked my husband to bring me our wedding cake topper to place on the cake because it desperately needed something to help it. I finished it on the first day so that I wouldn't have to think about it any more. I then set to work on my linzer tartlets, which came out perfectly. Maybe making them smaller was easier. Maybe it was luck. I'm thinking the latter was definitely the case. The chocolate truffles were a disaster. I tempered the chocolate exactly how we had spent an entire week learning to do. The truffles looked like something out of a magazine. In fact, I absolutely could not believe that I had made them. Unfortunately, they could not be picked up because the chocolate never set up. This, my friends is what happens when one tempers chocolate. I blamed the 95 degree kitchen that day.

Baking II is finally over and the really big surprise for me? My highest grade ever. It is time for Garde Manger, the class I have feared the most!

Patrice Johnson

CHEESECAKE
Yield: One 10" cheesecake

Crust: 2 cups finely chopped graham cracker crumbs
One half stick butter, unsalted, melted.

32 oz. cream cheese (room temperature)
1 cup granulated sugar
¼ cup whipping cream
1 teaspoon vanilla pure extract
4 eggs
1 teaspoon finely grated lemon zest

Mix crumbs with butter.
Line bottom of spring form pan with parchment paper and pan spray.
Press crumb mixture into bottom of spring form pan.
Wrap pan with two layers of heavy duty aluminum foil.

Combine cream cheese and sugar in large mixing bowl.
Mix for 5-10 minutes, scraping bowl sides frequently.
Add whipping cream and continue mixing until very smooth.
Add vanilla extract and lemon zest.
Add eggs and beat just to combine.
Pour cream cheese mixture into crust.
Bake in pre heated oven at 325 degrees in a water bath.
Place spring form pan in sheet pan and pour water into sheet pan so
that it reaches halfway up the sides of the spring form pan.
Check cheesecake after 45 minutes. Remove cheesecake when center
is still jiggly.
Take care not to over bake or it will crack.

CHEESECAKE VARIATIONS:

Black Forest: Add one cup semi-sweet chocolate chips to cheesecake
batter.
After pouring batter into pan, swirl in one cup of cherry pie filling.

White Chocolate/Amaretto: Add one cup white chocolate chips and
one third cup amaretto to cheesecake batter.

Butterfinger or Snickers: Add one cup chopped candy to cheesecake
batter.

Uncut - Chapter 25
We're Back in the Kitchen!

After 12 weeks of baking, we're going back to the "real food kitchens" and we're pretty excited! Even our class, with a perpetual sweet tooth is ready to say good-bye to cakes, ice cream and chocolate. It's time for Garde Manger. What you ask??

Pronounced Gar Mon Jay, it means to guard the food and it also refers to the cold kitchen. The words Garde Manger in French mean a cool, well aired storage place. Today, we know Garde Manger as the area of the kitchen, which is responsible for preparing cold foods.

The chef instructor is French (our first one!) and he is extremely serious about sanitation. In fact, he is Mr. Sanitation. Why? Because in the cold kitchen, nothing gets cooked. This is what makes proper sanitation absolutely crucial. Our chef instructor makes it quite clear from day one that he won't tolerate any licking of fingers to taste food, he absolutely won't let you in the classroom without a thermometer in your pocket, and you aren't going to get an A in his class. Okay, so at least I know what I'm dealing with. So far it is going about as I expected.

Now it is time for me to make a confession. Although I longed for those 12 weeks of baking to be finished, I have been dreading this class. From the first week of school we have been seeing the artistic works coming out of the Garde Manger classes and as a person who can't draw a stick man, I know I'm going to be in really big trouble. Any artistic talent is way out of the question for me!!

Within the first few minutes of class we are "creating" radish ginger flowers and roses carved from radishes and I'm thinking that my worse fears are now definitely confirmed. Radish carving is out for me. That becomes quickly apparent. But I'm in luck, because every week we'll be carving different vegetables. "Okay," I tell myself, "it's time to say good-bye to your "A" grade point average; this is definitely it." But just when I thought it couldn't get any worse, I found out about "the project" as I will fondly refer to it over the next six weeks of this class. In reality, the project has had many other names, but we don't want to go there! The project is a sculpture. Has this guy seen my radishes? C'mon, I can't sculpture my ponytail in the morning. Yet, we are supposed to create a sculpture out of chicken wire and then cover it with salt dough, tallow or weaver's dough. It's hard to believe, but it gets better. This project has to be mounted on a stand and become part of our final presentation. We have to decide what we're making and turn in a rough sketch (ha!), and, he has to be able to tell what it is! This is really going down hill fast! I can't draw a straight line with a ruler, so there is no way that I am going to be able to sketch anything, let alone create it in a 3-D format! I can't get a straight answer from my chef instructor on how building a sculpture relates to cooking, so I decide that I'm definitely not going to make it through Garde Manger. The fact of the matter is that the only food I'm going to be guarding is probably going to be my radishes since they are not fit to be seen by anyone.

The chef instructor warns us that we should not attempt to cover an existing sculptured piece with tallow. He will be poking a skewer into the piece to make sure that there is actual chicken wire underneath it.

After a few days, I pull myself together and I decide that I'm going to have a super positive attitude! I can make a sculpture. Sure I can! Fall is my favorite time of the year, so I decide that I will make a pumpkin and tie it in with a fall theme for my final. Piece of cake. Pumpkins are rustic and don't have to look perfect I rationalize to myself. These days

I'm doing an awful lot of talking to and answering myself. Relying on my past management skills for guidance, I decided to outsource the chicken wire armature to my husband who has an amateur talent for such obscure things. After attempting to cover the sucker (armature) with orange salt dough which has been dyed with turmeric (a spice) and made with tons of popcorn salt and cornstarch, I realize that this isn't working. The salt dough won't stick to the wire, which I've covered with gauze just like they told us to do. My nerves are rattled after three hours and the pumpkin basically isn't fit for the trash can. I decide to let the pumpkin "rest" for a few days and I think that maybe it will look better next weekend. I leave it at home rather than take it to my apartment for fear that I will smash it beyond repair if I bring it back with me.

Alas, when I return home the following weekend the salt dough isn't very orange anymore, it has formed big white bubbles, and here's the best part, it is cracking right off the chicken wire pumpkin. I'm ticked! If I can't make salt dough, I'm not feeling real good about weaver's dough (which is a bread dough). By the way, the chef instructor assured us that salt dough was the easiest medium, so basically I'm really in trouble now.

I have only one choice left and it is tallow. Now what is tallow you ask? Well, I'm trying real hard to forget about tallow these days, but it is white and classically made from animal fat and paraffin wax. It is pliable and easy to work with (by salt dough standards). I quickly mold a miniature pumpkin out of it in the classroom and decide this is definitely pumpkin material. That little pumpkin sits on top of my computer as I write this for you. My white pumpkin is quite a joke in our class (and I'm thinking that they'll really be laughing when they see it.) But I am acting like a chef now and with lots of confidence I inform everyone that there are white pumpkins; I've seen them! Do you remember Peanut's Linus waiting for the Great Pumpkin? Well it was white. Trust me.

Did the pumpkin ever make it to finals? Will I ever sculpt anything again?

Read on for the further sagas of Garde Manger! Can it possibly get worse?

What do you think??

Patrice Johnson

HOT CRAB FONDUE DIP
Serves 6-8 as appetizer

1 pound, crab lump meat
8 oz. cream cheese, room temperature
1 cup cheddar cheese, grated
4 tablespoons mayonnaise
1 tablespoon fresh lemon juice
1 teaspoon Worcestershire sauce
1 teaspoon dry mustard
¾ teaspoon garlic powder.

Mix cream cheese, mayonnaise, lemon juice, Worcestershire, mustard
and garlic in electric mixer until smooth and creamy.
Fold in crab meat and ½ of the cheese.
Pour into well sprayed casserole dish (shallow)
Top with ½ cup cheddar cheese.
Bake 350 degrees uncovered or until cheese is bubbly and casserole is
hot throughout.

Serve with lightly toasted baguette or crackers.

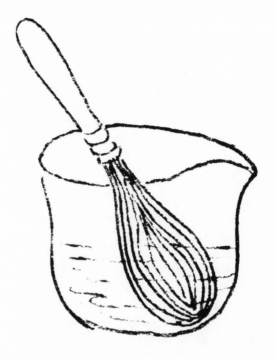

Uncut - Chapter 26
What's Hot in Garde Manger

We're in the cold kitchen, but now we're making chaud-froid platters. Chaud froid in French means hot-cold and guess what? We're back on the stoves!

Chaud-Froid platters are beautiful and normally are used for food presentation at fancy or special gatherings. They are also the source of that which has scared me since first seeing them during my first week of school. They are gelatin in consistency and have a béchamel base. Béchamel is basically a roux (flour and fat) mixed with milk and heated to make it thick. This makes a nice white base which is poured onto the bottom of a fancy silver platter. Not too difficult? No, but keep in mind that the béchamel must be at just the right temperature and it must be strained so that it is smooth. In addition, we have to make sure the platter is level before pouring to ensure a consistent thickness across the base of the platter.

I am telling all my friends that they would be super proud if they could see me now. Not only am I becoming a sculptress (with my pumpkin), but now I'm sporting a miniature level in my jacket side pocket! The bottom line is this: I've never used a level before and I looked at the bottom of those platters and thought they looked pretty darn level to me. I decide to just pour the béchamel. I am not a sculptor or architect and this stuff is starting to get a little ridiculous! The platter was obviously lopsided, one side too thick with béchamel, the other too thin. But why would this matter?

Because this is Cordon Bleu, right? It's got to be difficult. It's got to be perfect. Because now we are in for a special treat. We are going to take vegetables and cut them super tiny and very thin and place them on top of the béchamel to make designs. Yes, more art! Meanwhile we are carving turnips into sunflowers, but mine are being guarded with my radishes. There is no way I'm showing these carvings to the instructors. I search every night on the Internet for a place to buy pre-carved veggies, but I cannot locate such a service! I need to find this before finals when we will be required to do 15 carvings. I have no idea if such a service exists, but if it does, it would be well worth it to me to pay for it.

Now the béchamel has been evenly poured, and we're ready to place the vegetables. Did I mention that you can't touch the béchamel layer? If you do, your fingerprint will spoil it, so you have a one chance to place your vegetables and make your design. That is why I have a small pair of tweezers next to my mini level in my pocket. I place the vegetables down as carefully as possible, not touching the béchamel and thinking how this is so much easier than I had anticipated.

I'm actually surprised to see that my vegetables resemble flowers (unlike my carved ones) and I'm feeling pretty good about these Chaud-Froid platters.

The next step is to form a layer on top of the design to protect it. This is done by melting gelatin, cooling it to at least 90°F so that it won't melt the béchamel . Once the gelatin is at the proper temperature you strain it and then pour it carefully into a ladle and then onto the platter. If you let the gelatin cool too much it will begin to thicken and it won't pour.

I pour mine carefully onto the platter and watch the carefully placed vegetables begin to float all around the platter. That is about the time I hear the instructor say, "Now don't get frustrated, this is just our first time and we're going to be making one of these platters every week so that by finals you will have it down and it will be easy". Oh, I'm excited now! Not only do I have the great white pumpkin, but now I have floating vegetables in what used to be a pretty flower design. And we'll make one every week. What could be better than that? For one thing, we have to remove the air bubbles. This is done with a propane torch of which I am deathly afraid of. Never the less, I hold it gingerly above my platter and the air bubbles disappear like magic! One area of the platter becomes dark brown when I hold the torch a little too close to the gelatin layer.

The following week, I decided to try something different. I used some small cutters to cut pieces of the béchamel out of the white base. I then pour colored gelatin into the cutouts, let it set up and then covered the entire platter with a thin layer of gelatin. Guess what? It worked! Wow, I actually like these Chaud-Froid platters. But how is the pumpkin coming along?

Well, I can tell you this, it hasn't been smashed yet. Tallow is definitely my final choice and I'm trying to place it on the chicken wire and make it look like a pumpkin. At this point, you have to have a pretty vivid imagination to go there! The big question now, will it make it to the finals table?

ROASTED RED PEPPER & FETA DIP

16 oz. feta cheese, crumbled
4 tablespoons extra virgin olive oil
salt and pepper (to taste)
2 jalapeno peppers, chopped fine
2 pepperoncini,, chopped fine
3 tablespoons fresh lemon juice

Mix all ingredients together in food processor.
Let dip chill for several hours to become firm.
Serve with crackers or sliced baguette.

Patrice Johnson

Uncut - Chapter 27
Let's Make Sushi Cordon Bleu!

Sushi originated in China over 300 years ago, but the Japanese made it popular. It was used originally as a method of preservation. The Chinese made sushi from raw fish, which today is referred to as sashimi. Eventually, sushi (or sashimi) disappeared from China almost altogether. The Japanese began to eat the fish with rice, and sushi, as it is known presently, was reborn. Today, the sushi bar is the leading type of restaurant in Japan and is quickly becoming the most popular type of restaurant in southern California. I must admit that I have never frequented a sushi bar and I was shocked to see it here at my French cooking school! I decided right away that I would try to be brave and maybe even taste some. Maybe!

There weren't any women sushi chefs until the 1950's. This is because the Japanese believed that women's hands were too warm to handle the fish (remember our sanitation concerns, particularly if something isn't getting cooked). I think those Japanese women were maybe just a little ahead of their time and liked their fish cooked (like me!) If you're thinking that you might want to become a sushi chef, be sure you have plenty of spare time. It takes ten years to become a sushi master chef, and the first two years are spent just on the rice. I don't know about you, but being a potato person, I'm not sure I could spend two years cooking nothing but rice.

I've only been eating cooked fish for a few years, so the idea of eating raw fish does not appeal to me at all! Fortunately the chef instructor points out that I can actually try a cooked product; smoked eel! "Yikes," I thought. I don't exactly feel like having any kind of eel at nine in the morning. But now the entire class is taunting me and they have been trying all kinds of raw fish, and raw quail eggs, so I figure the least I can do is try some cooked eel. Guess what? It was good!

It was really fun making the sushi and sashimi treats and they turned out so attractive! We served them on slabs of multi colored marble to help keep them cold, but as far as tasting it, in the end, I decided I would quit while I was ahead. Leave my adventures for the day with the eel. If you ever wondered how sushi is really made and you don't have ten years to figure it out, here's the down and dirty. You take a piece of nori (seaweed) and place it on top of a really neat little bamboo roller. It looks like a miniature bamboo shade. Inside the seaweed, you layer rice (that food item you practiced making for two years), fish, vegetables and whatever else suits you. Then you use the bamboo to roll it tight. Voila! A sushi roll is born. Now all that's to be done is slice and eat. Making them is the easy part for me; actually eating it is another story. If you think eating eel in the morning is tough, the chef instructors had other good ideas for breakfast. Think caviar!

My Chaud-Froid platters are improving and I surprised myself and even the chef instructor by coloring the normally clear aspic that is poured over the top. I cut out a few leaves at the bottom of the platter and with my orange-brown colored aspic, it looks just like colors of fall. I know I'll have it down perfect for finals! My confidence level is high.

Today we had fun making quail deviled eggs. All I can tell you is to try this if you want a challenge, try making them. They are so tiny and I just kept thinking, who thought of this one???

Meanwhile, the sagas of the white tallow pumpkin continue! I was successful in getting it to stick to the chicken wire, but it looks lumpy and unlike any pumpkin I've ever seen. It isn't exactly the way I was picturing it! Can I smooth it out? Can I figure out a way to introduce some vertical lines in it like normal pumpkins have? Does it really matter since this isn't a real pumpkin in any sense?

SALMON CARPACCIO (Raw salmon appetizer)

Slice salmon very thin and flatten between plastic wrap to the
dimension of the toast points.

For each portion lay the salmon on a chilled plate and mount it on top
of a toast point.
What is a toast point? A small piece of bread which is cut out with a
cookie cutter and lightly toasted.

Serve with condiments:
eggs hard boiled and sliced or chopped
crème frâiche
red onion, brunoise(diced very small)
chives
capers

Patrice Johnson

Uncut - Chapter 28
Chef, Did You Really Say $65.00 Per Ounce?

Want to know the breakfast of champions? Caviar straight up on a gold spoon. It is 8:00 a.m, and I am still finishing my daily morning diet Coke. I don't usually eat much of anything until well after 9 a.m., so the thought of caviar has my head spinning. This class just keeps getting better and better.

The chef instructors are lecturing on caviar and how we are going to get to taste it! No expense has been spared; they got the "good stuff." They are commenting on how they hope we don't like it so that they can have our share. Now, I've never tasted caviar, but I'm feeling pretty confident about letting the chef instructor's have my share, on the other hand I'm thinking, "Maybe I will like it."

What is true caviar? Caviar is defined as the eggs of the female fish. Salted. That right there sounds so appealing, doesn't it?? These eggs are also known as roe. Now, for me, I like eggs from chickens only and I like them cooked! You may be interested to know that caviar has been around for a long time and it has always been a celebrated food. (except by me). It comes from the large bony fish known as a sturgeon. Today these fish are found only in the Caspian Sea. It takes 23 years to get the eggs from the sturgeon which is why caviar is so expensive. The average cost of caviar is $65 – $85 per oz.

Russia and Iran are the only two countries that produce caviar, with Russian production totaling the lion's share of 90%.

Caviar comes packaged in 2 kilo tins and is refrigerated for shipment. Once opened, it must remain refrigerated and will only last for three days.

Only "true" caviar is from the sturgeon fish. There are three true caviars:

1) Beluga — Largest sturgeon up to 15′ long, over 2000 lbs.
Maturity 20-25 years.
Eggs: biggest and most fragile.
Color of eggs: light steel to dark grey color.
Most expensive.
Sold in blue tins

2) Oestra — Up to 10′ long., 500 lbs.
12-15 years to mature.
Color of eggs: gold-brown.
Oily, strong, nutty flavor.
Smaller grains.
Less expensive than Beluga.
Sold in yellow tins.

3) Sevruga — Up to 7′ long, 150 lbs.
8-10 years maturity.
Color of eggs: Dark brown to grey.
Least expensive.
Sold in red tins.

Caviar is usually served with blinis or toast. It is served in its original container on ice with the lid showing. There is, it seems, a great deal of protocol that goes along with consuming caviar. The serving spoon is mother of pearl, bone or gold. Other spoon options are glass or crystal. But you definitely must not use metal or it will change the flavor and color.

The instructor makes us promise that we will at least try them all.

Hey, I've tasted eel; I can eat a little caviar, right? Being smart, I save myself a little diet Coke to swig, just in case. The chef instructor tells us that caviar is normally served with accompaniments like sour cream, which sounds to me like they are trying to cover up the taste. And when I tasted it I knew why! To say that an accompaniment was needed was quite an understatement! Other accompaniments to caviar are champagne and vodka; neither of which we had available. Believe me, I don't think that diet Coke was in any way the proper or appropriate accompaniment! I don't drink vodka, but I wanted some today!

We started with the lesser of the three caviars, Sevruga, followed by Oestra, saving the best, Beluga, for last. Now understand dear readers that true caviar goes for $65 - $85 per oz. and usually having expensive taste, I figure I'm going to love it. If you haven't sampled caviar, this is what I equate it to. Going swimming in the ocean and taking a big mouthful of water as the waves crash over your head. Since I'm sitting dead center in front of the chef instructor, he can't help but see the look on my face after the first spoonful. The Chef is stunned that I don't like it. "You really don't like it Patrice?" he said. "Chef," I say, "That is a major understatement." But he assures me that when I taste the Beluga it will be different. By the time I taste the Beluga, any available sips of my diet Coke are long gone and I'm maxed out to say the least. One thing I know for sure is that they all tasted the same to me. I'd rather be working on my pumpkin, so the fish in the Caspian Sea can relax!

Speaking of the pumpkin, we're only a few weeks away from finals and I am tired of working on the pumpkin. I decide that I need to bring it from my home to my apartment near school where hopefully now it will be safe from being smashed (but no guarantees). I bring it to my apartment hidden in a cooler and I refuse to even look at it. I have rationalized to myself that I have spent way too much time on the "project" and I now have to turn my attention to other things, like my homework, and my notebook for the class. It is based on this decision that I do not look at my pumpkin which is still safe, inside the cooler, for another two weeks.

Can I finish the pumpkin in time? Have I truly mastered the Chaud Froid platters, or can I take them to the next level?

Not in the mood for real caviar?

Patrice Johnson

EGGPLANT CAVIAR

1 large eggplant
1 large onion, chopped fine
3 tablespoons olive oil
5-6 large tomatoes
salt and pepper to taste
1 bay leaf
1 teaspoon sugar
1 teaspoon white wine vinegar

Bake eggplant whole in low oven at 300 degrees or until tender when pierced with a paring knife.
Sauté onions until soft.
Add chopped tomatoes and season with salt and pepper.
Add bay leaf and cook over low heat for 10-15 minutes.
Scoop flesh out of eggplant and chop coarsely.
Add onion and tomato mixture.
Heat in saucepan for 15 minutes. Stir frequently.
Remove bay leaf.
Process mixture in food processor until smooth.
Add sugar and vinegar.
Place in baking dish and bake for 30 minutes or until the mixture becomes thick.

Cool and refrigerate.
Serve cold with crackers or French bread slices.

Uncut - Chapter 29
The Great White Pumpkin

Do you know the history of English tea? It began as a tradition in the days of King George. He needed a 'pick me up' in the afternoon so tea and light sandwiches were served. It was not intended to be filling, but rather just to tide you over until dinner. Early tea was usually at 4:00 p.m., but sometimes was served as late as 5:00p.m. The Americans introduced the term "high tea," although they probably had no idea about the true history of tea served in the afternoon.

We made tea sandwiches Cordon Bleu style, which of course means they were all the exact same size and shape. We cut the crusts off our bread and used metal cookie cutters to shape the bread into diamonds and other fancy shapes much too beautiful to be handled. Once we mastered tea sandwiches we moved on. We made 75 lbs. of sausage in one day! Wow! I had heard that if you saw how sausage was made you would never eat it. Not true for me! Having made fresh sausage, I don't think I would want to eat it any other way. We ground all of our meats and seasonings ourselves and then used special sausage machines to stuff the sausage meat mixture, which is known as forcemeat, into the casings. Natural casings are the lining of animal intestines. There are also synthetic casings. Speaking of synthetic, reminds me of my pumpkin, and we definitely don't want to go there!

We used natural casings and I thought they would be disgusting, but they really were not. If you haven't seen them, I don't really know how to describe them except as white and a bit slimy. You must keep them wet so they don't dry out. Sheep casings are the smallest, hog casings next in size, and beef casings the largest. First we rinsed the casings with water and looked to see if any had sprung a leak. Next we filled the casings with the forcemeat and then tied them off into sausage links. The chef instructor had a special bin for the leftover sausage so we could send it to the production kitchen, but the more we grilled, the more we ate. The bins looked remarkably empty at the end of the day. My favorite sausage was the Mexican Chorizo! Our instructor said he was amazed that we had never made sausage. He said we looked like professionals. I thought, "I hope he is this impressed with my project next week at finals." Sadly, he informed us that we wouldn't be making any sausage for our finals. Our final menu items have yet to be announced, but for me the food is minor in the overall scheme of this final.

I've got the Chaud-Froid platters down pat and with finals a mere week away, I'm ready to go! This week on platter number four, I cut not only large leaves but an entire side of the platter with small falling leaves. They were so tiny that they were difficult to fill with the aspic, but I solved that problem by adding an eyedropper to my cadre of tools. It has a home in my pocket right next to my mini level. Filling them with the eyedropper worked out perfectly. With the exception of my pumpkin, my problems are over and I'm going to cruise through Garde Manger finals!

My "project", the pumpkin, continues to transform. It now has the vertical creases in it and is a little smoother than it had been before. I constructed a leaf out of tallow by flattening it with a rolling pin, then carefully cutting out a leaf. I added it next to the stem which I carved vertical lines in to make it look more realistic. Actually it's about as realistic as the Great White Pumpkin.

But with finals a week ahead, it is time to work on other things, such as my big fat notebook! I've got to give up on the pumpkin. What is done, is done! I am confident that my artistic Chaud-Froid platters will easily distract the instructor's attention away from the pumpkin!

My thoughts for next week:

Do finals go as perfectly as I planned?

Would there be some surprises or was it just another "ordinary" day at culinary school.

Is there any way I can ace this class?

On to happier thoughts, a recipe for one of my favorites!

BEEF WELLINGTON WITH MADEIRA REDUCTION SAUCE

10 oz. puff pastry dough
2 beef filets (5 oz. each)

Prepare the beef:
Season beef filets with salt and pepper.
Sear to rare on grill. Cool.

Roll puff pastry dough on lightly floured board.
Brush off excess flour with a pastry brush.
Place beef on top of puff pastry and add mushroom duxelle to the top
    of the beef.

Using the puff pastry wrap the dough around the beef as though you
    were making the beef into a package.
Use an egg wash (1 egg yolk, ¼ teaspoon kosher salt, and splash of
    water) to place on ends of pastry before putting them together.
    This will act as a "glue" to hold the dough.
Use a fluted pastry cutter to make the dough around the beef oval
    shape.
Using cookie cutters, cut out leaves or other shapes from excess
    puff pastry dough and place on top of the beef Wellington for
    decoration. Use egg wash to secure the dough pieces.
Brush the entire Wellington with egg wash and use a fork to pierce
    steam escape holes into the top.
Refrigerate until ready to bake.

Patrice Johnson

MUSHROOM DUXELLE

2 teaspoons unsalted butter
3 teaspoons shallots, minced
4 oz. mushrooms, diced very fine
2 oz. white wine or brandy

Melt butter in large sauté pan.
Add shallots and mushrooms.
Add wine or brandy.
Flambé.
Reduce to au-sec (dry)

MADEIRA SAUCE

4 oz. demi glace reduction
1 oz. Madeira wine
¼ stick unsalted butter (cubed)
Reduce stock by half to make demi-glaze.

Sauté shallots in small sauté pan.
Add Madeira wine and reduce to demi-sec (half the liquid)
Add stock and reduce again until the sauce is thick.
Taste for flavor and add additional wine and or salt and pepper as
    needed.
Taking the pan off the heat, swirl in cold cubes of butter until the sauce
    is thick and glossy.

Bake at 375 degrees for 20 minutes or until the puff pastry is golden
    brown.
Serve with Madeira sauce.

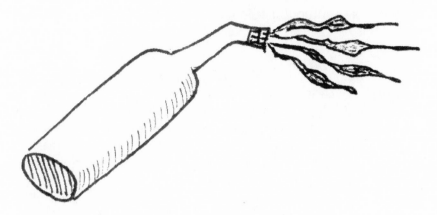

Uncut - Chapter 30
Garde Manger Finals. The Project Revealed.

This is it, another six weeks, another notebook, another final, and this time, "The project."

My Mom came to visit and insisted on seeing my pumpkin. She couldn't find it anywhere in my apartment. Aha! She had not looked inside the cooler! That is where my project belongs I assured her, in hiding. She laughed very hard when she saw it, which is a nice confidence builder for me as I go into my final presentation tomorrow. Thanks Mom! I had to agree with her, it is not right! But that isn't the half of it. Today at school, finals have already started and my chaud–froid platter is not working out as planned.

First of all, we are at assigned tables and the working space is very limited. I cut out my leaves as practiced for the last five weeks and they look okay, but then things start to go down hill, and I mean pretty rapidly. I made some aspic, colored it red and began using my eyedropper to fill my tiny cutout leaves. Yeah, you guessed it, the aspic dripped from my wonderful $1.99 eyedropper (which up to today has been working perfectly), and landed on the white béchamel base. This is the reason I bought an eyedropper, so this very thing wouldn't happen. I had to use a skewer to try to scrape the aspic from the béchamel. I'm sure you can imagine how successful that was since, as you might recall, you can't touch the base without marring it! I'm thinking that the colored pour layer (last layer) of aspic will cover up any mistakes. Sadly, that was my FIRST mistake.

There was no room on the table, so I took my platter over to the windowsill which is about one foot above the floor. Not taking the time to properly level my platter, I poured the aspic which immediately began to run like a roller coaster over to one side of the platter. You will recall that we use a propane torch to burn off any air bubbles that form on the surface of the aspic. Unfortunately, I had forgotten to bring one over from the other side of the room. By the time I return with it the aspic has begun to set up so I can't correct the off level problem by merely tilting it the other way. What's worse, the aspic has begun to pool and formed large clumps which I tried to burn off with the torch. Now, can it get any more perfect? Definitely! A school tour of potential students is walking by the window and they are totally fascinated with this little display, because let's face it, you don't see this kind of scene everyday. And I know the school representative is explaining that these students are in one of the more advanced classes! They stop to look in the window as I am calmly trying to use the propane torch to remove the bubbles. I'm pretty scared of the torch to begin with, so this makes it even more entertaining. At this point, the aspic is starting to burn because the torch is way too hot and it has been pointed on the platter ten times longer than it was supposed to be.

Next, "helpful" class mates are walking by and asking, "What happened? Your Chaud-Froid platters are always perfect." Now, I'm thinking these people don't have a clue, because I was really counting on this platter to save me from the pumpkin. But it gets better! We have to present 15 radish carvings. Are these instructors for real? My radishes can't be seen. They are being guarded. They certainly cannot be presented with the pumpkin and this completely screwed up Chaud-Froid platter.

I try to describe this scene to my Mom that evening and she laughs even harder (thanks again, Mom).

The next day, I carefully remove my pumpkin from its hiding place and put it in a box along with my other display items for my fall theme. I take my fall tablecloth and drape it over the top of the pumpkin because it isn't fit to be seen. In fact, last week I asked the chef instructor if I could make a private presentation so that nobody else could see it. Sadly, he told me to forget it.

With my pumpkin safely stored away, I begin to get my products out on the table and work on setting up my presentation. I was walking by a gorgeous Chaud-Froid platter which was getting its final torching to remove bubbles when I noticed that flames were shooting out of the propane torch's tank. The student quickly dropped the torch on the floor where it continued to burn. Another student yelled loudly, "Fire!" Our chef instructor came running over, assessed the situation and loudly announced, "Everyone, get out, run!" And, I have to be honest here, I'm thinking, "There is a God, the building is going to burn down and nobody will ever see my pumpkin, Chaud-Froid platter, or radishes." How lucky can I get?

My thoughts for next class:

Will we get to leave for the day?

Will the white pumpkin be gone forever?

The conclusion of Garde Manger.

RACK OF LAMB WITH ZINFANDEL SAUCE

1 rack of lamb, split and trimmed
1 tablespoon olive oil
salt and pepper to taste

ZINFANDEL SAUCE

2 tablespoons red currant jelly
¾ cup zinfandel wine
2 shallots, minced
2 teaspoons garlic, minced
16 oz. veal stock

Season and sear lamb to rare (internal temperature 120-125 degrees).
Heat jelly and wine and reduce by half.
Add shallots, garlic and veal stock and cook until sauce is thick.
Season and strain.
Spoon sauce over rack of lamb and serve immediately.

Patrice Johnson

Uncut - Chapter 31
The Garde Manger Finale

Although we had not yet to date had this particular experience in school, it seemed logical to all of us that when the instructor said "Run, get out!" he was probably pretty darn serious. Therefore, we all took flight! As I ran out of the classroom with everyone else, a classmate was walking down the hall towards the class. She was in tears because not only was she 15 minutes late (which equals a large deduction), but the salt dough sculpture of a large dragon which she was carrying was teetering and its wings were flapping as though they would fall off any second now. I managed to catch the dragon before it toppled to the floor and told her not to worry about being late. The dragon was magnificent! Surely, it was the best project here and I assured her that she should be thrilled that it wasn't going to burn up in the fire. In fact, I was considering offering her big dollars for the dragon because I figured

Patrice Johnson

I could just tell the chef instructor that the pumpkin hadn't worked out. And I'm sure that we can all appreciate how true that statement would have been. It was about this time that other students were offering cash as thanks to the student who had been holding the burning torch.

We are all hovering in the hallway waiting for our instructor to come out. I was trying hard to get a glimpse into the classroom and I was getting a bit nervous since I didn't see big flames licking upward towards the box which is holding my pumpkin. In fact, I didn't see any flames at all. I also noted, that the fire alarms haven't started going off yet, and we were all still in the building. Soon, a maintenance man rushes by with a fire extinguisher. No! I think, you're here too soon. My pumpkin hasn't caught on fire yet.

The chef instructor comes out a few minutes later and tells us that the fire is out, but the kitchen is full of chemicals from the fire extinguishers. This means they cannot taste any of our food since the chemical has been in the air. Gee, does this mean that maybe the chemicals marred my Chaud-Froid platter? Maybe they caused the aspic to have a pooled appearance. Do you think they might buy that one? At this point, I'm giving it serious consideration. My food was the ONLY thing I had going for me in the entire presentation. "What??" I ask the instructor as calmly as I can. You mean we aren't going home? I have to go back in there and set up my project?" Holy cow! If I had known this I would have taken the time to throw my pumpkin on top of that torch on my way out of the classroom.

To be honest, everyone was pretty shook up about the potential exploding propane torch, and I for one, intended to milk it for as much as I could. I was seriously thinking of claiming some kind of emotional trauma (which wasn't far from the truth) at this point.

I reluctantly went back into the classroom and finished my tea sandwiches, mini blue cheese éclairs, potato crepes with salmon and caviar, 15 radish carvings and my sliced galantine. Galantines I place about equal with making a chaud-froid platter, but we don't have time for those details here. I placed the fall items on my tablecloth, put out a few small real white pumpkins. This I did to create the realism that in fact, white pumpkins do exist. Lastly, I took the pumpkin out and placed it on the highest portion of my display. I draped the entire display with a garland of bright fall leaves, and believe me, this helped out considerably. I even lit my fall candles to add another dimension of light and to help remove focus from…well you know!

Then the best part of all came. We got to leave the classroom for two hours. Folks, if I was ever close to not returning to the classroom at anytime over the past ten months, this was the closest.

When we got back, the chef instructors seemed relieved that it was over.

We packed up our items, cleaned the classroom and went home. Grades wouldn't be given out until tomorrow.

Over the past six weeks I want you to know that I had devised several plans for exactly how the pumpkin would be destroyed. I thought of placing it in a campfire, or even more appealing, running it over with my car. In the end though, I couldn't do it. This pumpkin, this dreaded Garde Manger class, had become part of my life. I actually liked the pumpkin. (Just seeing if you would buy that.) The fact of the matter is, as you are well aware, the pumpkin played an integral part of my culinary career, not to mention an unbelievable conversation piece. I simply couldn't destroy it.

The next day, I packed my gloves to clean the classroom. Surprisingly, it was not to be. The "A" students got to cook instead of clean, and somehow through it all, from the chef instructor who doesn't give out "A's", I got mine! Tears were in my eyes. And it was with the greatest joy of my schooling to date, that I spent the morning with the other "A" students cooking a fine meal for our fellow classmates. The kicker though was when the chef instructor asked me during my exit interview why I didn't like my products. He said he thought they were great. I must have been stunned; in fact I know I was. Maybe I could have asked him how accurate his vision was, but I didn't want to know. I was excited beyond belief, International Hot foods, our last formal class is next!

I learned about dongas in my international hot foods class. I don't know where they originated, but they are similar to a donut and are easy to make. I think that you will find them to be a delicious treat!

Patrice Johnson

DONGAS (Donuts)

3 cups flour, all purpose
1 ½ cups sugar
1 tablespoon baking powder
1 teaspoon salt
1 cup milk
2 eggs
1 teaspoon vanilla extract.

Mix all ingredients together in a large bowl using a wooden spoon.
Dip an ice cream scoop in oil and make a ball.
Heat peanut oil in deep fat fryer.
Add dongas to oil carefully and fry until golden brown.
Dongas are done when a toothpick comes out clean.
Sprinkle with powdered sugar and serve warm.

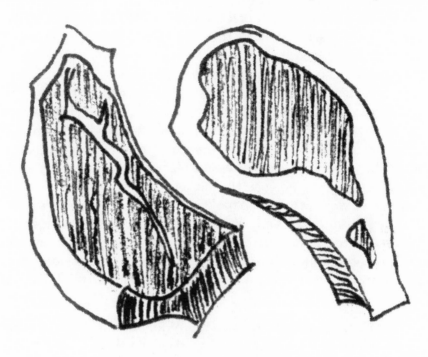

Uncut - Chapter 32
We're Seniors!

It's hard to imagine that culinary school started so many months ago, because it seems like just yesterday when we used to watch the students in the hot foods class with envy. They were the seniors; they were in their last formal class and from what we could tell, they made really good food. It doesn't seem possible that we are here now!

I have to tell you that the things we worried about in our early days seem very inconsequential now. The nerve racking tests of our knife skills, the constant written tests and the continuing test of our skills on product identification seem par for the course now. We're used to it! The pace in this class is going to make the other ones look like a picnic. I'm thankful that there are no three dimensional projects to worry about, so I think I'm going to be okay this time. I'm hoping for an easier six weeks even with the accelerated pace.

Patrice Johnson

We are all a little out of practice since we haven't been in the hot kitchen for 18 weeks. Personally, I thought it was pretty hot in the baking labs. I mean, ovens are hot, right? The average room temperature was 90 degrees which qualifies as hot. Anyway, according to the chef instructor (knower of all), we haven't been on the stoves for a long time and he said he can see how rusty we are. At that point I was so glad that this guy hadn't seen me nine months ago. In international hot foods we do a different country's foods each and every day. This begins with a lecture about those countries and then we use recipes as guidelines to prepare the dishes. The big difference: NO chef instructor demos! We've left the regimented world of following the chef instructor's demo plate exactly. The chef instructor reminds us daily that recipes are just guidelines. We have autonomy now to show our creative side and personally, I am excited, because I never knew I had a creative side until last term. But I know now that I do and so I'm not too scared. Compared to tallow, food is simple.

Today we are visiting the country of Russia and we are making Chicken Pojarski. What is Chicken Pojarski you may wonder! Well, it is chicken and veal ground up with the addition of seasoning and heavy cream. Now here's my favorite part. After grinding up the meat, the instructor tells us to shape it into little cutlets that look like miniature pork chops. Maybe it's just me here, but c'mon Chef! If you want a pork chop let's make pork chops! Why in the heck are we using ground-up chicken and trying to make it look like a chop? But before I can ask, it gets better. He instructs that we will take a piece of penne (tubular) pasta and place it into the "cutlet" to make it look like a bone. Now, personally, I'm thinking this is kind of a waste of time.

Chicken Pojarski is also served with a sauce, sans any weird additions. It is a simple paprika cream sauce. My partner and I are each trying to plate these little "chops" and they are sliding around the plate as if they are on ice. The chef instructor wants to see 'height', so we're trying very hard to stand them up against each other, but lets face it, gravity isn't going to allow it. Meanwhile the once warm plate is getting cold and the sauce is—you guessed it, breaking! To make it even better, we're late in our delivery and the chef instructor is yelling out "C'mon, I'm hungry." The funny thing about this Chicken Pojarski dish is that when we taste it, we discover that it is delicious. Maybe it is worth the effort of making it look like something it isn't. It even has the potential to look very good if we practice it about a hundred times. My partner is discouraged but I remind her that like the chef instructor told us, it's been a while since we've been in the hot kitchen. Seems like we weren't the only ones having problems. At the end of class we all had to remake paprika cream sauces together. Then we broke them on purpose (always easy for me to do) so we could practice fixing them. Our chef instructor is making these sauces look easy. He assures us that we'll have them down pat by the end of hot foods. Sauces are always a challenge so we are hopeful they will become easier.

PAPRIKA CREAM SAUCE

1 teaspoon shallots, finely chopped
1 teaspoon garlic, minced
1 cup heavy whipping cream
paprika to taste
parsley, chopped fine

Sweat shallots and garlic in butter in small sauté pan.
Add ¼ cup sherry to pan and reduce until almost all of the liquid is gone (au sec).
Add cream and continue to cook until the cream has thickened and reduced by half (demi-sec).
Taste sauce. Add additional seasoning if necessary.
Strain.
Swirl in cubes of cold butter until the sauce is thick.
Keep the pan moving while you swirl in the butter or the sauce will break.

This sauce goes well with any chicken or fish.

CHICKEN POJARSKI

Serves 4 as an appetizer

Equal parts 2 ½ pounds chicken breast and veal (ground)
2 cups heavy whipping cream
salt and pepper to taste
1 cup breadcrumbs

Patrice Johnson

Mix chicken and veal and cream together.
Season to taste with salt and pepper.
Shape chicken/cream mixture into small pork chops.
Dip in breadcrumbs and sauté in hot melted butter until browned.

Next chapter: We'll cook lobster, but there's a twist!

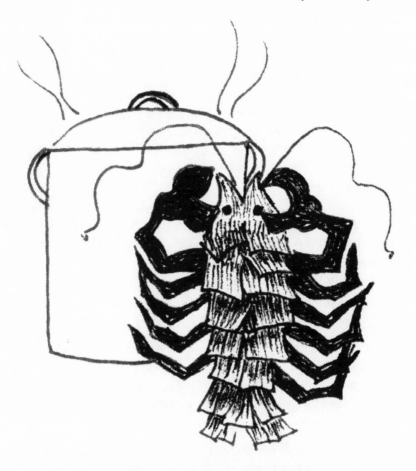

Uncut - Chapter 33
Let's Cook & Clean Lobster—
Cordon Bleu Style!

Today in hot foods we're going to cook whole Maine lobsters. They have been flown in just for us! Now, you all remember the last time we cooked lobster and the screaming lobster? Well, I was thrilled to find out at the beginning of class that the sous chef was going to cook all the lobsters for us today. We only had to clean them. The best news of all though, was that I lucked out and it wasn't my day to be the sous chef. Whew!

Now, if you cook lobster at home you may hear them "scream" when you put them in the pot. In some cases, that scream may just be a chef instructor being silly (like our Intro II instructor), but in the case that you do happen to hear it at your own home, here is the reason. You remember our chemistry classes from several months back, right? When the lobster is immersed in the hot water, the moisture inside the shell heats and turns to steam. Just like a teapot, the steam escapes which can make a screaming sound. But don't fear, the lobster isn't crying out in pain and you can feel free to enjoy your lobster without guilt. There have been many studies done about the most humane manner to kill a lobster. Some studies had students hypnotizing the subjects by rubbing their backs until they stood on their heads, others have tried putting them in the fridge before cooking to numb them up. I like the hypnotizing just because I'd really like to see a lobster standing on its head! The bottom line, most studies conclude, is that a few minutes in the freezer is the most humane for the lobster.

Remember that lobster meat can go bad quickly if it isn't immediately frozen, so it is important to cook a lobster while it is still alive. Never eat a cooked lobster with its tail uncurled, because that means that it died before it was cooked. In Cordon Bleu we place a skewer in the tail to keep it straight for presentation, so remember, things aren't always as they appear!

If you have always wondered what that green stuff is that you see inside the lobster: it is the liver. It is known as the tomalley and many people enjoy eating it. At school we saw a little tomalley magic. Our chef instructor made a green tomalley butter using the lobster's liver. He then placed the butter over heat and as it became warm it turned red. More chemistry folks! Who ever knew cooking could be this magical? Not only that, this class is actually fun! The fun part of school it seems, is finally arriving.

Speaking of enjoying lobster, here's a little twist for you. Our chef instructor showed us how to paralyze a lobster so it won't feel pain. After paralyzing the lobster, he cut it open and removed its heart which was still beating. Now, fortunately he had warned those of us who are squeamish, and so I also offer you fair warning if you wish to stop reading now! He then ate the beating heart! Just when I thought I had seen it all at culinary school!

My partner was feeling a little squeamish himself at this point and was in no mood to clean lobsters. He was willing to prep everything else that we needed to make our lobster with champagne sauce, so I gladly volunteered to clean the lobster. Since I grew up near the Chesapeake Bay, I've been used to cracking blue crabs since I was very young, so I considered this to be an easy task. We saved the lobster head and put it back on the plate along with the cleaned tail and the fanned shell end of the tail. In typical Cordon Bleu style, we made the sucker look whole again! The chef instructor talks to us about protecting the integrity of the food. C'mon now, we just killed a live lobster and you ate its beating heart, and now we're worried about its integrity? You know that I am not one to question, but gee, in Maine they are famous for serving you the whole lobster and wouldn't that be a timesaver? Of course, it would be, but here at Cordon Bleu we know that presentation is everything. I have to admit, that the plated lobster looked almost too good to eat. I had a bite, but somehow, it just wasn't as appealing to me as I had imagined. The champagne sauce was ultra rich and I was looking forward to making something else.

By the way, for you nutrition gurus, lobster is actually healthy with only 90 calories for 3.5 oz. IF you can eat it without the clarified butter. Lobster also contains omega-3 fatty acids which represent the "good" cholesterol which has been shown to reduce the hardening of the arties and decrease the risk of heart attacks. In addition to lobster surprises we are also cooking snails today. The chef instructor admits that most good French restaurants serve escargot, as snails are known in French. I have to give the French some credit for coming up with a cool name for these little slugs. In Maryland, I used to see these suckers on the sidewalk in the morning. The chef instructor also pointed out that most restaurants serving escargot are dark so that you can't see them too well. I heard that! There are of course special snail platters to hold them and we even had some fancy snail looking shells to place them in after they were cooked. (To preserve their integrity of course). This is a presentation style which totally eludes me! We made them covered in butter, the French solution to making everything taste absolutely divine! My partner insisted that they were very tasty, but for this culinary treat, I had to pass!

A long time ago lobsters were so plentiful that Native Americans used them to fertilize their fields and as bait for fishing. In colonial times, lobsters were considered to be poverty food. Not so today! My husband still regrets the day he gave me a taste of his lobster tail several years ago! It is said that large lobsters taste just as good as small ones until they get larger than 5 –7 lbs. when the meat becomes stringy. I don't know about you, but I don't routinely see five pounders!! If you prefer the tail meat like I do, buy a female lobster because her tail is broader than a male's of equal size since she needs extra room for carrying eggs. When you hear about a shellfish ban, you won't have to worry about lobsters. Unlike oysters, clams and mussels, lobsters are not filter feeders. Filter feeders pump sea water and any plankton or pollution it carries through their bodies. Any toxins in the water will be concentrated in their flesh. Lobsters, crabs and fish don't filter plankton from sea water, so they are safe during outbreaks of red tide.

What is Red Tide?

Red Tide is caused by a "population explosion" of toxic, naturally occurring microscopic plankton Explosions or "blooms" are coastal phenomena caused be environmental conditions which promote explosive growth. Factors which are especially favorable include warm surface temperatures, high nutrient content, low salinity and calm seas. Rainy followed by sunny weather in the summer months is often associated with red tide outbreaks. Red tide actually does change the color of the water in coastal areas can be colored red by the algae, thus the term "red tide." Although toxic blooms often turn the water reddish brown, many nontoxic species or reddish brown plankton cause the same discoloration. Conversely, toxic plankton may be numerous enough to toxify shellfish, but not sufficiently abundant to discolor water. Discolored water should always be regarded with suspicion. When red tide occurs, some seafood is unsafe to eat. Only a few marine animal s accumulate these toxins. Shellfish, are particularly prone to contamination as they feed by filtering microscopic food out of the water. If toxic, planktonic organisms are present, they are filtered from the water along with other nontoxic foods.

Filter-feeding shellfish include quahogs, soft-shell clams, oysters, mussels and scallops. Since toxins are stored in the digestive tract (stomach) of these shellfish, scallops are safe to eat as long as only cleaned muscle meat (the only part generally eaten) is consumed. Whelks and moon snails can also accumulate dangerous levels of the toxin during red tide as they feed on contaminated shellfish. Lobsters, crabs, shrimp and finfish do not accumulate toxin and are safe to eat from affected waters.

If you are wondering what to do with all those lobster bodies you have leftover after cooking your lobster, we made something which I think you will find excellent! If you want, you can add pieces of lobster meat to make it richer.

Typically the word bisque refers to a cream soup made with shellfish in the world of classical French cuisine, but these days you will notice that lots of soups are referred to as bisques.

SHELLFISH BISQUE
Serves 4

2 lbs. lobster shells
1 stick unsalted butter
¾ cup carrots, diced small
¾ cup celery, diced small
¾ cup onion, diced small
¼ cup brandy
3 oz. tomato paste
1 tablespoon paprika
4 black peppercorns, cracked
2 bay leaves
1 teaspoon thyme
1/2 cup flour
2 cups clam juice
2 cups vegetable or chicken stock
2 cups heavy cream

Bake lobster shells until they turn bright red.
Crush the shells with a mallet.
Place the lobster shells in a saucepan with butter and cook until
    caramel in color.
Add carrots, celery and onion to the saucepan.
Cook vegetables until they are tender.
Add brandy and flambé. Be sure to say loudly flambé!
Add tomato paste, paprika, peppercorns, bay leaves, thyme, and flour.
    Stir constantly.
Add clam juice and stock and simmer for one hour.
Puree in blender and strain.

Patrice Johnson

Return to stove, finish with 2 cups heavy cream and adjust seasonings
   if necessary.

You may garnish this soup with sautéed shrimp and chives if desired.

CHAMPAGNE SAUCE FOR LOBSTER

2 shallots, minced
2 tablespoons unsalted butter
2 teaspoons garlic, minced
3/4 cup clam juice
1 vanilla bean, split
1 cup heavy cream
3/4 cup champagne

Sauté shallot in butter until soft.
Add garlic, champagne, clam juice, vanilla bean and heavy cream.
Simmer on low heat to infuse the vanilla flavor.
Strain sauce.
Taste and adjust seasoning if necessary.

Serve with lobster.

Uncut - Chapter 34
It's Tapas Time (Spanish Happy Hour)

Have you ever been to a "tapas" bar? You probably have! Tapas originated in Spain and are usually served before dinner. Tapa time in Portugal is like "happy hour" here.

Speaking of happy hour, here is a fun story about some of our classmates. The president of our school had requested that we not wear our school uniforms out in public, particularly to bars. He was not of the opinion that this is the appropriate image for the school. One night several students went out to a local bar for drinks. While there, they noticed a student in his Cordon Bleu chef's jacket. He was not from our class and they didn't know him. He was obviously drunk and enjoying himself quite a bit on the dance floor when they spotted him. The room was dark and he couldn't see them from where he stood.

Every so often they yelled out "Hey, look, it's a Chef from Cordon Bleu". He looked around frantically each time this happened, but he never could spot them. They continued to chant "Hey, it's Cordon Bleu!", until the poor embarrassed student left the bar. The next day in school, this story was relayed and throughout the day we shouted "Cordon Bleu!" using the highest shrillest tones we could master. This sing song phrase stuck around until our very last day at school. The chef instructors never figured it out, and although I wasn't there, I couldn't help but picture that poor student on the dance floor that evening.

Tapas came to be in the nineteenth century. During that time there weren't any paved roads or trains in the rural countryside of Spain. There were lots of bandits and robbers and traveling was very dangerous. Tired travelers were frequently looking for safe places to rest and have a glass of sherry and so they stopped at small Inns along the way. Upon their arrival, innkeepers would rush out to greet the travelers bringing cold glasses of sherry or red wine. Local taverns used to serve the sherry and guests would place bread slices on top of their glasses in between taking sips to keep flies out of their drink. Somewhere along the line, a bartender placed a piece of sausage on the bread and tapas were born! Soon, the bread was replaced with small plates.

These days any type of hors d'oeuvre is known as a tapa. In Britain they call them starters, Americans know them as appetizers. Tapas in Spain come in two sizes, small and not so small. The small dishes are usually a few bites so that you don't spoil your dinner appetite. These tapas are usually served cold directly from the bar and are considered to be the "true tapas." A larger dish about twice the size is usually served hot.

For our tapas we prepared squid. Squid is part of the octopus family. They can range in size from one inch all the way up to 80 feet. The meat is known for being firm with a chewy texture and a mild, sweet flavor. Squid is popular in Asian and Mediterranean dishes and in Japan it is used raw in sushi. Squid is more commonly known as calamari, probably for obvious reasons! I'm sure you can appreciate my excitement over preparing the squid. The thing I never knew about squid is that they have ink sacs! The ink can be extracted from the sacs and used in food to provide a dark black color. We used the ink (which fortunately had already been removed by someone else), to color our pasta a dark black.

This dish is known as Calamares en su tinta, which means "squid in their ink." It is popular in Spain. The ink has no flavor and it won't stain your teeth which is kind of a shame since I was going to use that ploy as an excuse for not tasting it! Actually, the dish looks very attractive with the dark squid, a few lemon slices and some croutons. For those of you who want to try your hand at this dish and are wondering where to buy the squid ink, you can probably find squid at an Asian supermarket. How you extract the ink, I don't know, but it may make a fun science fair project.

African cuisine is becoming more popular recognized international cuisine. Agriculture is the main economic activity in Africa. One thing that makes the dishes of Africa rather unique is that many of their meals combine a sweet and savory flavor in the same dish. They use lots of fresh and dried fruits. They combine meats, fish and vegetables all together into a single stew. A traditional salad is composed of oranges and olives.

We learned that they do not have much beef on their continent. This is because the tsetse fly infests over 1/3 of the continent and this affects their ability to raise cattle. As a sort of alternative, a very popular item in Morocco is rabbits, which we also prepared. This was my first time preparing rabbit and I have to be honest here, I couldn't help but remember my pet bunny, Mr. Whiskers. As you might have guessed, I couldn't deal well with the taste of the rabbit although everyone agreed that it tasted like chicken. I kept seeing Mr. Whiskers wiggling his nose at me.

Usually in Morocco people sit on the floor to eat using large cushions. Belly dancers entertain the guests at the end of the meal. We, of course had no belly dancers performing for us at school! Morocco, we learned, has a lot of peanuts. In fact, Africa is the #1 producer of nuts in the world. We actually made an African peanut soup. Next best thing to having some peanut butter on a spoon.

I thought you peanut butter fans might enjoy a taste of the African peanut soup, so let's go Moroccan style!

Patrice Johnson

AFRICAN PEANUT SOUP
Serves 8

1 large onion, finely chopped
2 cloves, garlic, minced
1 teaspoon cayenne pepper
1 teaspoon Indian curry powder
2 tablespoons peanut oil
2 tablespoons Garam Masala*
3 cups chicken or vegetable stock
8 tomatoes, concasse**
2/3 cup peanut butter
salt and pepper to taste
4 tablespoons sour cream
8 lime wedges

Sauté the onion, garlic and cayenne pepper in oil or butter.
Stir in the curry powder and heat for a few minutes.
Add the chicken stock and tomatoes, simmer for 10 minutes.
Strain and then blend.
Return to the stove and bring to a simmer.
Add the peanut butter by whisking it in and seasoning with salt and
    pepper.
Garnish with sour cream and lime wedges.

Chef's note:
If you want to go over the top here, as we did in school, place your sour
    cream in between two spoons and try to make a quenelle. This is
    a three-sided football shape which looks very pretty as a garnish,
    but it does take some practice.
*What is Garam Masala and where can you get it?
Garam is the Indian word for hot. Garam masala is a blend of dry
    roasted ground spices (up to 12 of them). It can include black
    pepper, cinnamon, cloves, coriander, cumin, cardamom, dried
    chilies, fennel, mace, and nutmeg. You can actually find it in most
    grocery stores.

*What is a tomato concasse and how do I make it?
Boil water. Place your tomato in the water for 30 seconds.
Shock it in ice water. Peel, seed and chop. Now you, master Chef, have
    tomato concasse!

Uncut - Chapter 35
The Perfect Luau, Pacific Style

Many of you have enjoyed the foods of Hawaii. Did you know that Hawaiian food comes from a combination of American, Japanese, Chinese, Portuguese, Korean and European cuisines! No wonder it is so tasty! Hawaii cuisine incorporates fresh fruits and vegetables, macadamia nuts, seafood and meats. A trademark dish of Hawaii is a plate lunch, which is sometimes called a mixed plate. Essentially it is a boxed lunch. It is usually a blend of Japanese, Hawaiian and Chinese food for the entrée which consists of fish or meat and it is served with two scoops of sticky white rice and a scoop of macaroni salad. Kind of different to serve two starches together, isn't it?

Those who live in Australia call their country "lucky". In the world of cuisines this is particularly significant because Australia has an abundance of food. They are fortunate to have many exotic fruits and large varieties of fish. Some of the best beef and lamb in the world are produced in Australia. Asian cuisine has a major effect on their culture.

Today is going to be especially fun for our class because we are going to prepare a buffet lunch using recipes from both of these two countries. It has been several months (all the way back to Intro II) since we have prepared a buffet. This one will be for all of the other classes in the school and since we are now the "seniors", this is our chance to shine. We have all attended this luau buffet lunch before and we want ours to be the best ever!

We had a great time preparing the food and we didn't have any major disasters or problems. Months ago I may have considered seeing one of our classmates walking with a paper towel on fire a problem, but at this point we've seen it all. That is why we are all pretty much nonplussed when the firewalker passes us by on his way to the sink to extinguish the lit towel. As he walks, the fire is being fanned by the movement of air and the flame which is getting larger is now licking his hand. After putting the towel in the sink he walks over and shows me his arm. All of the hair has been burned off of it! The chef instructor is oblivious to all of this and we just laugh. Apparently someone had left the towel on the stove where it caught fire from one of the pilot lights. Normally when this happens we place the towel on the floor and stomp it out. In the ideal kitchen, we don't leave paper on top of pilot lights nor do we walk with paper which is on fire. Oh the safety classes seem so long ago.

When the food was served we looked at it with pride and I heard several students comment that it was quite an improvement over the first buffet we had prepared. The best part was tasting the food, which was excellent. We all agreed that our culinary skills had improved a great deal since that first buffet. This stuff was actually edible!

You may want to host a luau sometime, so I've included some recipes for you to try. In Hawaii they often make poi, which isn't usually a big hit with us, mainlanders! Poi is a starch dish which is made from cooked, peeled and mashed taro root which has been allowed to ferment for a day or so before it is served. Poi has been a major staple in Hawaii for hundreds of years. We didn't make poi, but instead sliced the taro root thinly and deep fried it. It tasted like a really good potato chip, so you may want to try some. Taro root is commonly available in Chinese markets. We also made sweet potato chips, an excellent option if you can't find that taro root.

LOBSTER SALAD WITH SOY DRESSING

1 tablespoon soy sauce
2 teaspoons honey
1 teaspoon fresh ginger, minced
1 lime, juice and zest (chopped fine)
1 tablespoon olive oil
2 whole lobsters

Heat soy sauce, honey, ginger and lime zest in saucepan.
Simmer for 2 –3 minutes.
Add lime juice and remove from heat to cool.
Whisk in olive oil.
Cook lobsters and extract meat.
Place lobster meat into mixing bowl and add the soy dressing.

Serve on a bed of lettuce leaves of your choice and mix together.
Easy and impressive!

KAHLUA PORK LOIN

2 lb. pork tenderloin, boneless
1 cup soy sauce
1/2 cup dark brown sugar
2-3 tablespoon garlic, minced
2 teaspoons fresh ginger, minced
1 teaspoon kosher salt
½ t. ground black pepper
¼ cup vegetable oil

Marinate pork in soy sauce, brown sugar, garlic, ginger, salt and pepper
overnight. Sear pork loin on hot, well oiled grill. Roast pork at 375
degrees until the internal temperature is 145 degrees. Remember,
meat will continue to cook (carry over cooking) after you remove it
from the oven. Avoid overcooking the pork or it will be dried out.

Patrice Johnson

GRILLED FRUIT KABOBS

Pineapple, cut into chunks
Mango, cut into chunks
Star fruit, sliced
Plantain or banana (if using plantain, par-cook it first)

Thread fruit onto wooden skewers, which you have soaked in water for
at least 45 minutes. This will prevent them from burning.

Make a glaze for the fruit and brush it before grilling. Your glaze can
be anything at all from citrus juice and honey to a light coating of
olive oil flavored with citrus juice and citrus zest.

Aloha!

Uncut - Chapter 36
Germany & Great Britain

A common joke at our French culinary school was that the English can't cook! In general, the French feel that way about all other countries, USA most definitely included! This week we are learning how to cook food from Great Britain, Scotland and Wales.

The British are known for their crumpets, scones, sausage, mustard, fish and chips and other pub food. They also have some wonderful cheese. They are most famous for their British breakfast which is prepared all together in one skillet. The Brits are also famous for many of our modern day Christmas traditions like Christmas cards, caroling and fruitcake.

I don't know about you, but I've always wondered what the heck a crumpet is! They are similar to a small pancake but are made with yeast which makes them a little more puffy than a pancake. They are cooked on a griddle but only on one side.

Patrice Johnson

Our main course today was a wonderful venison shepherds pie. I had never tasted venison, but found it to be similar in taste and texture to beef. The meat is a very dark red and quite lean compared to beef. The recipe lends itself well to being made with beef as a substitute, so I will share the recipe with you and you can modify accordingly in case your hunting adventures are not successful.

The countries of West Germany are well known for their love of cooking, eating and drinking beer and wine. During the middle ages luxurious banquets were common. They displayed whole lambs, calves and deer brought to the table covered in ornate gold and silver. These events lasted for hours. Germany is well known for its beer palaces, some of which have over 100 menu items! We made the famous sauerbraten which I was surprised to learn is marinated for 4-5 days. No wonder it has such a powerful flavor.

This is a great meal which can be prepared ahead of time. It is hearty, so I would consider serving it with something light such as a salad. You can make a large pie or individual portions. Let's make venison Cordon Bleu!

VENISON SHEPHERD PIE
2 servings

1 tablespoon pork fat such as salt pork (or substitute bacon)
8 oz. venison meat chopped into large cubes (or substitute beef round steak)
2 celery ribs, small chop
1 small onion, small chop
½ cup mushrooms, thinly sliced
2-3 tablespoons garlic, minced
1 teaspoon tomato paste
3 cups brown veal stock
½ cup mashed potatoes
2 tablespoons sharp cheddar cheese, grated

Brown seasoned meat in fat. Add celery and onion and caramelize. This means that you want the vegetables to take on a deep brown color. Keep the heat low and take your time until the vegetables are dark brown in color. Add mushrooms and brown. Add garlic, thyme and tomato paste, and cook for 3 minutes. Next, add hot stock one cup at a time and simmer mixture slowly for about 90 minutes or until the meat becomes very tender.

Assemble the pie in a shallow dish. Place beef mixture on bottom of dish and then add mashed potatoes on top of the beef and sprinkle with the cheese. Season if desired and brown the potatoes in the 400 degree oven for about 10 minutes.

Mashed potatoes can be spooned on top of the beef or piped through a pastry bag for a fancier presentations.

Lesson: Mother Sauces. There are 5 mother sauces which are considered to be the base of making all other sauces. They are: Béchamel, Espagnole, Tomato, Hollandaise and Veloute. Today we will learn about Béchamel sauce.

At school we use the mother sauce base of Béchamel to make a cream sauce, known in French as sauce crème. Begin with onions cut very small (brunoise) and sweat them in equal parts butter and flour (roux). Stir constantly and cook for about 10 minutes. Season with a pinch of nutmeg. Slowly incorporate milk or cream. Simmer for 30 minutes being careful not to burn. From this mother sauce of Béchamel you can go on to make macaroni and cheese, by adding any type of cheese that you want along with your cooked noodles. Wait until you try this! You won't be able to eat macaroni and cheese out of the box again!

In this case, to make a sauce crème, add only cream. Quickly sauté your spinach leaves (no more than 30 seconds) and then add them to your sauce crème. Don't forget to season your sauce crème with salt, pepper and a little nutmeg. Now, you have made a wonderful creamed spinach! This is also a nice side dish to any meal.

Patrice Johnson

Uncut - Chapter 37
The Middle East

The cuisine of the Middle East includes, Greece, Turkey, Syria Iraq, Israel, Iran, Egypt, Lebanon and Jordan. Nine nations, one cuisine. It is like no other in the world. Middle Eastern cuisine features exotic dishes that are vivid with spices. Greek food traditionally centers around vegetables, fish, seafood, olive oil and lots of fruit.

Greece and Turkey are known for shish kebabs, spanakopita, phyllo, stuffed artichokes and tomatoes, fried pastries and baklava. The Arab states are also known for sweet glazed nut such as pistachios and walnuts.

We used the skills we learned in baking to make pitas, which we combined with a wonderful, home made hummus. Hummus is relatively healthy and when served with pita bread makes what is know as a "complete protein". This means that if you want to eat vegetarian style you can eat this complete protein and it will be equal to having meat or fish. Pita is the bread of the Middle East. Pita bread is used primarily as a utensil to scoop up food. Traditional pita bread does not have a pocket.

Patrice Johnson

Hummus is so simple that it would be the perfect dip for an unexpected guest. If you want to try an easy hummus dip for summer time fare, I think you will find that it goes great with crackers and vegetables also. The nice part about the dip is that you can easily keep these ingredients on hand.

Let's make hummus and pita bread Cordon Bleu!

HUMMUS DIP

Combine in food processor: 2 cups of chickpeas (garbanzo beans canned with their juice); combine with 2 teaspoons salt, 1 head of roasted garlic, lemon juice, Worcestershire, and Tabasco to taste and 1 cup tahini.

Finish with ground cumin and olive oil to taste.
The mixture should resemble a smooth puree.
Sprinkle with paprika before serving.

If you really want to impress your guests, make your own homemade pita bread. It isn't hard to do!

PITA BREAD

2 ¼ cups water
½ oz. active dry yeast
pinch sugar
8 cups flour, all purpose
3 teaspoons salt
¼ cup olive oil
1 cup flour

Mix liquid ingredients first and then add dry.

1. Dissolve yeast in water.
2. Add olive oil.
3. Add flour.
4. Add salt.

Knead until it bounces back. Approximately 10 minutes.

Shape into a ball and let rest for 45 minutes in a warm place until double in volume.

Punch down and divide into 8 balls.

Roll out ¼"-1/8" (thin).

Keep turning the dough as you roll. This will keep it nice and round. You want small circles.

Let the dough rest on a board sprinkled with cornmeal **uncovered** for 20 minutes so that the dough will form a skin. This skin will create a pocket.

Bake at 450ºF in the oven for 3-5 minutes.

Do not brown.

Oven spring will rip the bread open and this will cause it to puff up as it bakes (forming the pocket). Remember, oven spring is what happens when the yeast hits the oven and your bread rises up. In this case, it provides the action you need to make the pocket.

TANDOORI CHICKEN

1 large onion, chopped fine

6-8 garlic cloves, minced

3-4" ginger, chopped coarse

4 tablespoons lemon juice, fresh

8 oz. yogurt, plain

1 ½ tablespoon coriander, ground

2 teaspoons turmeric, ground

2 teaspoons cumin, ground

½ teaspoon mace, ground

½ teaspoon nutmeg, ground

¼ teaspoons cloves, ground

½ teaspoon cinnamon, ground

4 tablespoons vegetable oil

1 ½ teaspoons salt

1 teaspoon black pepper

½ teaspoon cayenne pepper

1 tablespoon yellow food coloring

1 tablespoon orange food coloring

10 chicken breasts, bone in or boneless

Patrice Johnson

How to make the Tandoori marinade:

Using food processor chop onions, garlic and ginger.
Add lemon juice and blend.
Place ingredients into large bowl and add remaining ingredients.
Mix.

Place chicken in marinade and refrigerate overnight, turning
    occasionally.
I place my chicken in a zip lock bag for easy cleanup.
Grill chicken on hot grill and baste with the marinade as you grill it.
Serve chicken pieces with lemon wedges.

Uncut - Chapter 38
Mexico, the Caribbean & South America

Most Mexican people here in the U.S. will tell you that they do not find their style of cuisine in our Mexican restaurants. They will tell you that they think our Mexican-American version of their food is too heavy. Authentic Mexican food is lighter and features lots of fresh fruits and fresh herbs. Traditional dishes are flavorful but normally mild. For those who like food hot, as many Mexicans do, a spicy sauce is served on the side. Tortillas made from corn or wheat flour are popular all over Mexico and are considered to be a staple of Mexican cuisine.

Traditional Mexican food is served with a smaller amount of meat or chicken than we are used to seeing. Sour cream and cheese, which we almost insist on with our Mexican food, is an American restaurant innovation!

In Brazil fiesta and carnivals are a huge part of their culture. Fiestas of course have lots of food! Brazil is fortunate to have bountiful natural resources and rainforests. Tropical fruit is also plentiful. Brazil is known for restaurants known as a churrascaria which is a place specializing in spit-roasted marinated meats that are served to order in the rodizio style. This style means that waiters travel through the restaurant carrying skewers of meat. When they come to your table they slice as much as you want from the skewer. Typically diners order several types of meat, which are served with salads, rice, black beans, french fries and collard greens.

Popular choices for food in Brazil are pigeon, duck, rabbit, deer, and wild boar. The most popular of all is guinea pig. Fortunately we aren't going to be making any guinea pig Cordon Bleu style! Not that I would have been entirely surprised if we had.

In Jamaica, food is rich and spicy and originated with the Taino Indians. Jamaican cooking is a melting pot, which combines Spanish, English, French, Indian and Chinese with a hint of African influence. This combination helps to make the food of the Caribbean very creative and different. Jamaica's history tells the story that maroons on the run had to come up with a way of spicing and slow cooking pork, which came to be known as "jerking". Today, jerk chicken and fish are popular also.

In Puerto Rico cuisine is also traced back to the Taino Indians who had a diet of tropical fruits, corn, wild meats and seafood. Spaniards added beef, pork, rice, wheat, garlic and olive oil. Africans brought okra and taro.

Fruits, nuts, corn, peppers, and ginger play a major part in Caribbean cuisine. Jamaica grows the entire world's supply of allspice! I don't know about you, but I used to think that allspice was a combination of different spices. In fact, allspice is a pea size berry of the evergreen pimiento tree. In Jamaica allspice is known as Jamaica pepper. The dried berries are dark brown. The spice got its name because it tastes like a combination of cinnamon, nutmeg and cloves.

The culture and cuisine of the Caribbean features a fresh abundance of local seafood. We cooked an unusual soup made with coconut milk and a more traditional black bean soup with a bit of ham.

JERK CHICKEN

5 pounds chicken, chopped
3 habanero chili peppers (if you can't get habanero, substitute
    jalapeno peppers)
3 garlic cloves, minced
1 tablespoon fresh ginger
1 teaspoon nutmeg
1/4 teaspoon cinnamon
1 teaspoon allspice
1/8 teaspoon cloves, ground
1 teaspoon whole black peppercorns
2 tablespoons kosher salt
½ bunch green onions, chopped
½ onion, chopped
1/8 cup vegetable oil
2 tablespoons brown sugar
1/8 cup lime juice
1/8 cup white wine vinegar
1/8 cup water
¼ cup dark rum

Puree all ingredients in food processor.
Marinate chicken for one hour and grill. Be sure to baste with marinade
    as jerk marinade has a tendency to burn quickly.

Easy, impressive and excellent!
Serve it with some black beans for some true Caribbean summer style!

BLACK BEANS:

2 cups black beans, dried
3 tablespoons olive oil
½ large red onion, diced
1 large green bell pepper, diced
½ medium jalapeno pepper, chopped fine
2 large garlic cloves, minced
4 tablespoons cilantro, minced
salt and pepper
2 teaspoons cumin, ground

Patrice Johnson

Soak black beans over night or boil in water for 10 minutes, remove
    from heat and cover.
Soak for one hour.
Heat olive oil in saucepan.
Add vegetables and jalapeno and sauté until soft.
Add garlic, cilantro and beans.
Cover beans with water.
Bring to boil, reduce heat to simmer.
Simmer for one hour or until beans are very tender.
Add salt and cumin to taste.

TORTILLA SOUP

2 tablespoons olive oil
1 large onion, chopped fine
8 roma tomatoes, quartered
2 oz. Ancho chile, dried, rinsed, seeded and cut into small pieces
2 tablespoons chile powder
2 teaspoons oregano
8 cups chicken or vegetable broth
one package corn tortillas, cut into strips
lime juice, fresh to taste
2 chicken breasts, cut and cubed (optional)

Heat oil in large pot over medium low heat.
Add tortilla strips and cook until golden brown.
Add onion and garlic.
Cover pot and cook until onion is very soft.
Add tomatoes, chilies, chili powder and oregano and cook until
    tomatoes are soft.
Stir in chicken broth.
Cover and simmer until vegetables are all very tender
30-40 minutes.

Puree soup in blender and return to pot.
Add lime juice to taste and serve with fresh lime wedges.

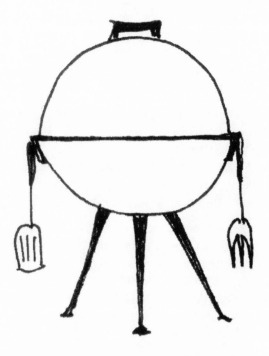

Uncut - Chapter 39
Southeast Asia, China and Japan

Our chef instructor told us today about his visit to China. It seems that everywhere he went he had a really great Chinese meal and always inquired about why there were no fortune cookies. Everyone gave him odd looks when he asked. When he returned home, he learned that Chinese fortune cookies are an American tradition! What we do know about the food of China is that Confucius taught the Chinese people to respect good food and thereafter standards of how food should be eaten were established. Even today the family sits down together to eat and discuss their day and this is way of life to the Chinese. In the U.S. there are actually five types of Chinese cuisine. Cantonese is food from the southeast, Mandarin is from the northeast, Hunan is from the central regions, Szechwan is from the west and Fukien is from the eastern coast. Canton is the port, which was first visited by the most people from the Western world and is therefore is the most common Chinese food cuisine. Dim sum is Cantonese and represents the tea and snack tradition.

Japan has a total land acre of 1,458,835 and therefore is huge. The country consists of four main islands. The presentation of Japanese foods had much to do with the development of power of Zen Buddhism and it evokes a spiritual attitude toward cooking which dictates that attention be focused on one thing at a time.

Mirin is a low alcohol, sweet golden wine that is made from glutinous rice. It is a popular ingredient in Japanese cuisine. It adds sweetness and flavor to a variety of dishes, sauces and glazes. Is also frequently referred to as rice wine. Another common Japanese ingredient is Miso, which is a fermented soybean paste. It is developed by injecting cooked soybeans with molds. Doesn't that just make you crave some Miso??

Fish is a staple in the Japanese diet. Did you realize that there are seven types of salmon? Do you think we had to memorize them?? You bet! So, for some interesting trivia conversation you can impress your friends and family the next time you make salmon. Be sure to tell them that you know that Atlantic means farm raised. Tell them that King, Chinook, Silver, Chum, Coho and Copper River are other types of salmon. Ask which one is their favorite!

Teriyaki has been with us for about 50 years. The recent craze for Japanese food has been due in part to our acceptance of sushi. Since fresh sushi is hard to come by in the desert, which is where I live, we'll go with teriyaki. Let's add some beef teriyaki to your summertime grill— Cordon Bleu style of course!

BEEF TERIYAKI
Serves 2

1 ½ lb. lean boneless beef sliced into ¼" slices

MARINADE:

3 cups soy sauce
4-5 cups granulated sugar
6" piece of ginger, minced
1 head of garlic, mashed
3 bunch scallion's sliced
1 cup Mirin or sherry
sesame oil to taste

TERIYAKI SAUCE:

1 tablespoon sesame oil
1 head garlic, mashed
6" piece of ginger, mashed
1 cup pineapple juice
2 cups soy sauce
2 cups chicken stock
4-5 cups sugar
½ cup cornstarch
½ cup sherry
water (only if sauce is too thick and you need to thin it.)

Pierce beef with fork and marinade for 1-2 hours.
Make the sauce by sautéing ginger, garlic, and sesame oil.
Deglaze the pan with pineapple juice and cook until the liquid has
    reduced by half.
Add the rest of the ingredients, bring to a boil and then simmer.
Thicken with a slurry.

What is a slurry? A slurry is a thickener with equal parts cornstarch and
    liquid, in this case the liquid is sherry.
Strain and keep warm.
Serve with steamed rice and grilled summer vegetables such as
    eggplant and yellow squash.

TERIYAKI PORK CHOPS
Serves 4

2-3 garlic cloves, minced
½ cup soy sauce
3 tablespoons mirin or cream sherry
3 tablespoons cider vinegar
2 tablespoons dark brown sugar
2 tablespoons grated ginger root
4 pork chops (boneless)

Combine garlic, soy sauce, mirin and vinegar in a small saucepan.

Bring to a boil. Add brown sugar and gingerroot and cook until the sugar is completely dissolved.

Cool marinade.

Season pork chops with salt and pepper.

Place pork chops in large plastic bag and marinate overnight.

Grill chops on hot grill until cooked through.

Tip: If you want to save time on the grill, mark your chops with grill marks on both sides and finish baking in a 375 degree oven. You may also mark your pork chops ahead of time and then bake them off later.

SESAME CRUSTED SALMON

Brush salmon filets with extra virgin olive oil.

Toast sesame seeds until light brown.

Coat salmon with sesame seeds on both sides.

Sauté salmon is olive oil on medium high heat, flipping once.

Today we went on a field trip! Why? To learn about Southeast Asia! The countries, which make up Southeast Asia which we studied, are Thailand, Vietnam, Malaysia, the Philippines and South Asia.

No, we didn't get to board a plane and visit these countries; we simply headed down the road to one of many southern California Ranch 99 markets. Ranch 99 markets specialize in Asian products, which can be hard to find in regular supermarkets. We were required to spend at least one hour in the store. I was there for well over two hours. I've never seen anything like it! There were large tanks full of any kind of fish you can imagine! There were also tanks with lobsters, clams and even Maryland blue crabs. The meat department was equally fascinating with any animal part you can imagine. The frozen food section had all types of popular Asian steamed rolls/breads and appetizers ready to be re-heated in your microwave.

My absolute favorite though was the bakery. A popular item in Southeast Asia cuisine is purple yams and they are used extensively in baking. The bakery had the most vibrant purple cakes you can imagine and also very brightly colored pastries. These pastries do not resemble anything you see in our bakeries! I even saw some purple yam ice cream.

One of the students purchased some purple yam cake and purple yam ice cream, which we sampled in class the next day. Excellent flavor!

Coconut milk is common in Southeast Asia cuisine. Other popular items are lemon grass, palm sugar, shrimp paste, fish sauce and chilies. All southeast Asian societies have substantial Chinese and/or Indian immigrant populations. Rice and noodles are the main staples. They serve very little meat and dishes revolve around the staples. Fish is abundant.

Spring rolls are an adoption from Chinese cuisine. Unlike the Chinese, the Vietnamese do not deep-fry their spring rolls. We made spring rolls using fresh vegetables, marinated tofu and spring roll wrappers. It was relatively easy since we had already made them once before in Garde Manger. This time however, the spring rolls needed to be presented on a plate with a beautiful mint and cilantro dipping sauce. I made the spring rolls easily, cut them on a diagonal and then tried to decide how to plate them. If I laid them down flat on the plate they would begin to unroll and they also looked awful and unappetizing. Somehow, I needed to get them to stand up. I needed to make them look like Cordon Bleu rolls! I balanced three of them together standing in the center of my plate. Then, I placed the mint/cilantro sauce all around them. They looked great, except for one small problem. They would not stand up on their own. I placed some lettuce leaves underneath them and hoped that would give them some leverage and make them stand easier. I asked my cooking partner if she thought is was likely that I could ask the chef instructor to come look at them at my workstation instead of trying to carry them across the room to him. We agreed that wasn't likely, so I carefully picked up the plate and did my best to get them up there while they were still standing. The chef instructor was most impressed with the presentation (and so was I considering gravity hadn't kicked in yet). I quickly snapped a picture for my notebook before he ate one. Southeast Asian cuisine was unfamiliar to me before school. I found that I really love it! For those of you who are also fans of Southeast Asian cuisine, I have a fun recipe for you to try! Let's make Thom Kah Gai Soup from Thailand.

Patrice Johnson

THOM KAH GAI SOUP (Chicken & Coconut)
Serves 2

2 cups water
1/4 cup fish sauce
15 oz. coconut milk
2 green onions, chopped fine
1 teaspoon fresh ground ginger
1 stalk of lemongrass, sliced thinly
2 Serrano chilies, seeded and chopped
2 limes, juiced
2 boneless chicken breasts cut into 2" strips
2 oz. mushrooms, sliced
1 tomato concasse (chopped medium dice)

In a saucepan bring the coconut milk and water to a boil.
Add chicken pieces, lemon grass and ginger.
Bring to simmer.
Cook for 20 minutes or until chicken is cooked.
Add mushrooms and chilies.
Simmer for 10 minutes.
Add lime juice and fish sauce and serve immediately.

Garnish with tomato concasse.

Uncut - Chapter 40
Italy

Everyone seems to love Italian food! Italian cuisine, both northern and southern was invented by the Romans. They had a liking for strong, often redolent tastes, anchovies, fruity olive oils, sardines and pickled oysters.

Italian cuisine can be divided into two categories. The Italian food we in the United States are most familiar with is the cuisine from southern Italy. In the south of Italy, the population is poor. There is little industry there; mostly textiles and mining. The north of Italy is entirely different. The cuisine there is similar to Greek and Mediterranean food. Seafood is very popular in both regions due to their close proximity to the sea.

Patrice Johnson

We learned that in United States, we use pasta as an excuse to eat sauce. We pile it on and cover it with meatballs, sausage and mounds of grated cheese. In Italy, pasta is served with little sauce and the sauce tends to be light. Sauce becomes the flavoring element in the dish, not something to smother the dish.

We made an excellent Stracciatella soup. Stracciatella means "little rags" and this soup is frequently known as Italian Wedding Soup.

We also made pasta and used some of the squid ink to color it black. We made another batch of pasta and colored it using saffron infused water. Now we had black and yellow pasta dough. We rolled these out to resemble a "tiger" and filled them with rock shrimp ravioli. Very impressive, but making pasta does take some time. Also, don't forget that you need to get that squid ink!

BEEF/ITALIAN SAUSAGE LASAGNA

1 pound lasagna noodles, cooked
2 pounds mild Italian sausage, removed from casings and crumbled
1 pound extra lean ground beef
2 large onions, diced small
4 cloves garlic, minced
4 tablespoons extra virgin olive oil
2 tablespoons oregano leaves
2 tablespoons Italian seasoning
3 tablespoons basil leaves
¼ cup sugar
3 bay leaves
2 cans diced tomatoes in their own juice
2 16 oz. tomato paste
1 cup burgundy wine
salt and pepper to taste

FILLING:

16 oz. Ricotta cheese
16 oz. Cottage cheese
2 eggs
1 pound mozzarella cheese, grated
½ pound parmesan cheese, grated

Sauté onions in olive oil. Add garlic and sauté for one minute, stirring constantly.

Add sausage and beef and brown.

Drain fat.

Return beef and sausage to large pot.

Add spices, tomatoes, tomato sauce and wine.

Simmer for 2-3 hours on low heat.

In a large deep baking pan 13x9" (sprayed with pan spray) begin layering with sauce, spooning enough to cover the entire bottom of the pan.

Next, add a layer of lasagna noodles.

Add meat to top of noodles followed by filling.

Sprinkle cheese on top.

Repeat layering two more times.

Finish with meat sauce and top with shredded cheese.

Spray a piece of aluminum foil with pan spray and place on top of the lasagna.

Bake 350 degrees, covered for 1 hour, 15 minutes.

Remove foil for last 15 minutes of baking to brown cheese.

After removing from oven, let lasagna cool for 10-15 minutes before cutting.

A large metal spatula works best to get the lasagna out of the pan in a clean piece.

Serves 12

Enjoy.

Patrice Johnson

Uncut - Chapter 41
Born in the USA

Now that we have talked about all the other countries it's time to bring it home with our very own USA! Does the U.S. also have traditional cuisines? American cooking has been shaped and influenced by many different things. Early French, English and Dutch colonization, the black influence in the south and the pioneer traditions in the West. Other contributors were the immigrants of central Europe to New Jersey, Pennsylvania and the upper Mid-West. We have also seen influences from the Greeks, Portuguese, Asians, Italians and Basque. Our culinary melting pot probably represents the most complex melting pot in the history of food, because we have such a variety of cuisine. The cuisine of the U.S. is usually categorized by region.

New England is known for their clambakes and lobsters. Virginia is best known for its smoked ham and bacon while Gumbo is popular in New Orleans. You may have heard of Philadelphia Pepper Pot, which is a famous soup from you guessed it, Philly! Almost everyone knows about good old Philly cheese steaks!

I've told you all about those famous Maryland blue crabs so you are familiar with the Baltimore specialty crab cakes. There is southern style cornbread, southwestern style crab cakes and of course blackened catfish with black-eyed peas, collard greens and sweet potato chips from the South! California cuisine is known for some of the more trendy dishes that appear on menus, such as Cioppino, prawns, heirloom tomatoes, and seared duck breast.

We are nearing the end of hot foods, which also marks the end of our formal classroom training! These days we are presenting our food in what the chef instructor likes to describe as "restaurant day". We do this about once a week and it is actually fun. The goal is to serve identical plates to the instructor all at the same time and all looking precisely the same. To accomplish this, we work as a team because in fact we have several courses to prepare; each one must contain the 15 identical plates!

The instructors assure us that this is very important since frequently customers see a plate delivered to a neighboring diner and they decide to order it. If they don't get what they saw on the other customer's plate, they get very upset! Consistency is the key. It is easy now for us to plate one or two dishes on our own, but this requires a very different set of skills. We now have to work together and rely on each other for the timing of the plates. For the most part this is relatively easy, although now a bunch of chefs are trying to agree on how to make everything look artistic on the plate. Each of us has a very different idea!! You know how persnickety those Chefs can be!

In the end, we relish restaurant day because it is fun and it also takes the pressure off of us all individually. Our last day of restaurant day is really fun because we split our team into two and actually serve the other team. What an unusual concept it is to actually sit down and have a meal at culinary school! My husband laughs because I tell him that I have spent my hungriest days in culinary school! This, he says makes absolutely no sense. For me, cooking all day diminishes my appetite, and in addition, who has time to eat??

I thought you may enjoy a recipe for classic Cioppino from San Francisco.

CIOPPINO
3-4 servings

2 tablespoons olive oil
1 small onion, small dice
2 ribs celery, small dice
¾ cup fennel, small dice
4-5 garlic cloves, minced
½ cup white potato, peeled and diced into medium cubes
1 cup dry white wine
1 tsp dried thyme, oregano, rosemary and basil
1 bay leaf
8oz. tomato sauce
2 oz. tomato paste
6 oz. canned pear tomatoes
32oz. clam juice
2 pounds assorted fish cut into cubes and shellfish such as clams or
    king crab
½ pound shrimp
½ pound scallops
Kosher salt and pepper to taste

Sauté onions in olive oil. Add fennel, celery and garlic
Add herbs and wine and reduce to demi sec (half-dry).
Add potatoes and cook until soft.
Add tomato sauce, tomato paste, and clam juice and bring to a boil.
Lower heat.
Simmer for 30 minutes or until the flavors of the herbs have infused
    the broth.
Add fish and cook until done (when shells pop open)
Adjust seasoning and garnish with chopped parsley, grilled bread or
    croutons.

Note: If you want the soup thicker, add 2 tablespoons cornstarch
to hot broth, stir well to dissolve. Return thickening liquid to pot. Bring
broth to boil and then simmer until thickened.

Patrice Johnson

Uncut - Chapter 42
The Ultimate Final

The moment of Final 500 has arrived! This is it; after countless finals, this is the one that ends it all. The thing that makes final 500 so special is that there are a possibility of 24 items to make and they weren't selected for their ease of preparation. In fact, these menu items are among the more difficult things that we have had to prepare over the past 11 months and here is the kicker; we walk into the final with **NO** recipes. The menu consists of an appetizer or soup, an entrée and a dessert.

Over the past several months I have been a relatively mellow test taker, but for today's final 500, it was not to be. I woke up early even before my alarm, feeling pretty calm. We didn't have to be there until 10:00 a.m. which feels like noon to me. I decided that morning that even though I had been practicing the possible 24 combinations for six weeks that I didn't remember anything. I spent two hours memorizing the menus again and this didn't do much for my now frazzled nerves.

By the time I arrived to the school campus and saw my best friend, I could feel tears welling up in my eyes. This was just too much; I couldn't do it. She took one look at my face and quickly raced to her locker and

Patrice Johnson

offered me a shopping bag filled with more special tools that I may need. I added these to my collection of two bags packed full of tools and reminisced about the once skinny knife roll that I used to carry. My tools have been expanding at the rate of about one per week and for final 500 I packed up everything from my kitchen at home just in case! With the addition of the shopping bag, it was doubtful whether I could make it upstairs without a wheelbarrow. I had previously considered bringing one, but I had the feeling that wouldn't be well received by the chef instructor. My friend assured me that once I got in there, I would be fine. Even though she had not yet taken the 500, I took her words to heart.

When I was in my first Intro class (a lifetime ago), my chef instructor told us how fast our time at school would go. He said that he is always amazed at how quickly he sees his Intro students coming in to take the final 500. When I walked in and saw him, I remembered his words and couldn't believe that I was actually here! He asked me how I was doing and I told him that I was uncharacteristically nervous. He had an evil grin on his face.

We selected our menu items from a bowl and when I saw mine, I breathed a small sigh of relief. These were things which I had recently made at home and so I set to work. The pace was incredible; there wasn't a spare minute. I decided that I must begin with the dessert since it would take the longest. My game plan was to make one course every hour. We could serve our food whenever it was finished, however it had to be served in the appropriate order (appetizer, entrée and dessert). I felt pretty comfortable once I started to work. However, I can't tell you how shocked I was when the chef instructor informed us that two hours had gone by. Holy cow! Yikes! I hadn't served him anything. I noted that nobody else had either. I quickly plated my appetizer which was salmon carpaccio on brioche toast points. When I took it up to him, he had an approving look on his face and I began breathing again. One down, two to go. I was talking to myself and answering. I convinced myself that surely I was going to pass this final. Incidentally, the actual final grade is only for your own information on the final 500. This grade does not play into your final grade point average. However, you must pass the final 500 to graduate.

Things were going fine with my dessert. I had already piped my éclairs, baked them and made the pastry cream to fill them. The pastry cream was setting up in the refrigerator which was why it was critical to make it early.

Meanwhile I worked on my salmon entrée. This was a complex dish which wraps a piece of salmon in a brioche dough which is layered with mushroom duxelle, rice, hard boiled sliced eggs and asparagus. Unfortunately, my dough had been out in the hot kitchen for too long and consequently it was sticky and difficult to work with. I floured the dough and remembered this very same chef instructor telling me in Intro class that everything can be fixed. Determined to make it look good, I patched it back together as well as I could and even cut out a fish shape from the dough and placed it on top. I brushed the whole thing with egg wash and placed it into the oven to bake. Next, I needed to concentrate on the saffron cream sauce. Folks, you know that if I even look at a sauce, I break it, and I had decided that I absolutely could not break it today! In fact, at this point I was using sports psychology techniques which I have read about, to help me through the remaining minutes of this final. I have heard that athletes visualize themselves crossing the finish line of a race, or picture themselves winning a gold medal in their Olympic event. This focus allowed me to picture myself making a difficult sauce and not breaking it. It was probably this thinking which made me feel inclined to begin talking to my sauce. I remembered with fondness my international hot foods instructor and how he taught us to make cream sauces. He taught us how to fix them if they broke and I was prepared to use those techniques here. However, today, it was not to be. I made the perfect cream sauce. I plated the salmon entrée, cut it in half, and stacked it high to achieve the ever popular Cordon Bleu height requirements. Then I placed the saffron sauce along the front of the plate, drizzling a small amount on top of the salmon. I was talking to it the whole time and begging it not to break. It was a beautiful sauce and as I took it to the chef, I was thrilled that I still had 15 minutes to finish the éclairs. Naturally I had been working on them in between the completion of the salmon and sauce.

The éclairs were served with a strawberry sauce and it wasn't as cold as I wished it to be, so I had placed it in the freezer prior to assembling the salmon entrée. Lucky for me, it had not frozen solid.

The deduction for being late is one point for every minute and with 30 seconds to spare, I decided that the éclairs needed to be presented. I took them up to the Chef who by now was surrounded with lots of things to taste.

I walked back to my station and took my first drink of water in three hours. I was in a complete sweat. My hands were shaking. Deep down I knew I had passed. The sauce alone had to have done it for me.

Next we cleaned the kitchen and it was wonderful mindless work. My friend offered me a taste of his chocolate mousse which we enjoyed with some of my leftover strawberries and sauce.

The chef instructor left the room and came back with our printed grades. He told us that if we didn't pass we should arrange to take the test again and of course it would cost $200 for the pleasure of repeating the experience. I thought to myself, there is no way I could mentally come in here and do this again. Naturally, I was the last one to receive my grading sheet. The chef instructor smiled at me and shook his head, but I knew he was joking. I looked down at the paper saw the 94% and felt weak.

Thanks Chef I said as I walked out the door. My, I thought. What an incredible, unbelievable year it has been. I'm thinking of the challenges of the last year and realizing how much I have learned and how different I look at food now. But at this moment, it is all I can do to get my gear out of there and run down the stairs to search for my friend.

SALMON IN BRICOHE DOUGH (Kulebiaka)

Dough: You can make your own brioche dough or use phyllo or puff
    pastry.
These doughs are available in the freezer section of the grocery store.
I used puff pastry for this exam and it worked pretty well.

2 ½ pounds salmon
½ stick unsalted butter
1 tablespoon shallots, minced
½ pound mushrooms
½ cup white wine
 salt and pepper to taste
2-3 cups white onions, sliced
½ cup long grain white rice
1 cup chicken stock
3 hard boiled eggs, sliced
2-3 dill sprigs

Filling: Rice (cooked), mushroom duxelle, hard boiled eggs (sliced) and pieces of dill.

Roll out puff pastry dough on a light floured surface.
Brush dough with melted butter.
Add salmon to the dough, top with rice and mushroom duxelle.
Brush edges of dough with egg wash (egg yolk, water and salt)
Fold dough over to enclose the salmon.
Pat edges tightly together so that they will not open when it is baked.

Brush dough with egg wash and pierce with a fork to vent. Bake in oven preheated to 350 degrees.
Your dough should be a golden brown. This should take 15-25 minutes to bake depending on your oven.

Note: See chapter 29 for mushroom duxelle instructions.

Patrice Johnson

Uncut - Chapter 43
Dining Out

My husband and I frequently go out to dinner on the weekends to try new restaurants. Occasionally when my Mom visits she and I will go out to try a new place. At the moment though, nobody wants to go out to eat anywhere with me. They say that I am totally ruining the dining out experience for them. One thing I know now as the end of culinary school approaches, is that you can never go back. I know that I will never be able to go out to eat again without looking for the things which I have been conditioned to see on the perfect plate.

I remember fondly now our sanitation instructor who asked us kindly not to show up at restaurants with our instant read pocket thermometers to check the doneness of our meat. We would never! But, would I reposition my husband's plate in front of him so that it is facing the way the Chef intended instead of the way it was placed by the server? Have I totally rearranged a quesadilla so that the points form a design rather than look at it in its haphazard configuration on the plate? Do I ALWAYS feel the temperature of the plate and make sure that it is streak free? Do I constantly analyze the seasoning of the food and try to determine what is in it? YES to all!

Fast food is almost out of the question for me now, although I'm not beyond ordering a pizza after a long day. I still crave really good burgers, although none seem to compare to those we made in school with the addition of pork fat.

I take food apart layer by layer to see how it is constructed. My niece was recently enjoying an apple tart until I dissected it and told her all of the things that weren't right about it. And for heavens sake why are people serving ice cream and other plated desserts without a cookie? Where is the crunch?

To this day I cannot serve a plate without wiping it clean first. Presentation skills are ingrained in me forever.

The Top Ten Best Tips I learned at culinary school.

1. Don't over cook food—remember the carry over cooking principal.
2. Parchment paper—use it all the time!
3. Pan spray- it is mandatory!
4. Seasoning—the real secret to gourmet food. Don't forget to add it, adjust it, and taste your food. This is the untold secret of professional chefs.
5. Everything can be fixed (well, almost everything).
6. Recipes are only guidelines. Vary them. Don't be afraid to substitute an ingredient.
7. Stock—the real secret to excellent sauces.
8. Safety—food and personal. Don't ever forget it.
9. Organization. Make lists for your parties. They will save you time!
10. Don't sweat it, it is only FOOD!

Uncut - Chapter 44
Front of the House

If you thought we had fun in the kitchen, you should see us now! Not only is it our last two weeks of school, but we are going to spend them in the "front of the house." For those of you wondering whose house we are in, it is the school restaurant.

Front of the house in the restaurant industry refers to that area where we have not been. It is basically the opposite of the back of the house which is the kitchen.

Most of us are not looking forward to spending time in the front of the house. One student in particular keeps telling the instructor that he should not be here. He is adamant that he belongs in the kitchen and no where else. The instructor sighs as he obviously hears this every two weeks and he is sick of it. Front of the house is not an option. It is a mandatory portion of our program and with two weeks left to go we have to bite the bullet and go for it!

Every day we spend a few hours in lecture. This means we talk about how to greet guests, how to answer the phone and make reservations on the automated reservation system, and how to open and pour wine. Pouring wine is something we all know we will enjoy. At last we have reached the point of the program where I know I can master something! However, unlike our wine class where we got to actually sample wine, that is not the case here. Too bad, because most of us are in a very celebratory mood!

Each day at 10:30 a.m. we have what is known as family meal. Family meal is basically cooked for us by other students who are now doing their restaurant rotation portion of the program. This is probably one of the highlights of being in the front of the house.

Promptly at 11:00 each day the chef comes out to describe the days specials and to show us how they look when they are plated. Each of these we must memorize so that we can recite them to our customers. The customers at the restaurant come there because it is a good opportunity to sample inexpensive gourmet food and to see the students in action. Some of them obviously enjoy this and are definitely there for the entertainment value, while others, it seems, probably wish they had made a different choice for lunch!

Each day we work with a real waiter or waitress (i.e. someone who has a clue) so that we can see how to do things the right away. Some days we describe the specials and take orders, while other days we serve drinks, bread, and sometimes even the actual meal. About one week into our front of the house tour we are starting to feel like we know what we are doing. Except for one student who has been avoiding serving all week and now has been informed by the instructor that his time to serve has come. He was a nervous wreck and continued to beg to be removed from this assignment. As I was heading into the dining room I saw him proudly carrying a large tray of drinks. "He's doing great," I whispered to my friend. He began to take the drinks off of the tray to serve his table of four. You have probably already figured out that he has never done any serving prior til today. Therefore he wasn't prepared for the tray to go off balance when he removed the first drink. It almost looked like slow motion when the remaining three drinks tipped over the edge of the tray and onto the back of one of the women at the table. She had on a very sheer silk blouse which was instantly drenched and even more sheer. At this point the rest of us were trying to control ourselves since we were being trained to act appropriately in an elegant, upscale restaurant. I immediately excused myself from the restaurant and went to the café next door. It was there that I was doubled over when my best friend found me. "What are you doing?" she asked. "Oh, my," I said, taking out my notepad. "I need to capture this moment!" When I stopped laughing and returned to the dining room, I saw the woman with the drenched blouse coming out of the restroom. Folks, I'm sure I don't have to tell you that she wasn't looking real happy!

It was at this point that the poor embarrassed student said to the instructor, "I told you, I don't belong out here. Please, just let me back into the kitchens."

SERVING WINE PROTOCOL

Bring the bottle to the table before opening it.
The bottle should rest on a white napkin or towel as the label is shown
    to the guest.

When the guest approves the wine, open the wine following the
    correct procedures; hold the bottle, cut the foil top and peel it
    away, wipe the cork and the bottle rim with the napkin or towel,
    insert the corkscrew and twist until it holds, then pull the cork out
    and place it at the right side of the guest who ordered the wine.

After the cork is removed, wipe the rim again.

Allow the host to sample a small amount of the wine.

After the host approves fill the wine glasses of all the guests a the
    table. The proper amount per glass is 2/3 full. Do not fill to the top!

Know what to do if the host does not approve the wine.

The wine bottle should be placed at the right of the host's wine glass.
    If the wine is red, no ice bucket is necessary. If the wine is white it
    should be placed in wine cooler.

Patrice Johnson

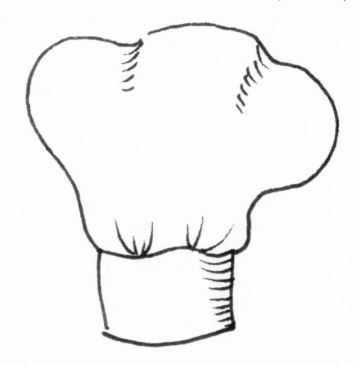

Uncut - Chapter 45
Good-bye to Culinary School

Today is starting out just like every other school day. I am pressing my uniform and getting my tool kit ready. Today, however, is not the same. It is the first day of my externship! It seems hard to believe that last week this time my fellow students and I were counting how many hours of school were left. Now, I'm longing for the security and comfort that I found inside the walls of the school. Last week as we left the school campus after exactly one year, we felt a great deal of frivolity, but also a deep sadness. The last day of school was filled with teary good-byes and fond remembrances of our year together. Many students are staying in southern California, but for me it was also a good-bye to the place which I have called home for the past year. It was most definitely a bittersweet good-bye, because I have enjoyed my time at school and my time in southern California. I am longing to return to my home though, and I know that this is the beginning of my journey to get there.

We have developed close, lifetime friendships; an aspect of school that I never considered when I ventured there one year ago. Our class had a huge party to celebrate our success. At the school, our class was known as the one that was much different from the other classes. We were known for having more enthusiasm and a wonderful camaraderie with each other, which the chef instructors told us was quite unique. We had some laughs about the tough times we had encountered over the last year. I think the burning torch won the prize for our favorite story. We perused pictures of one another in the classroom, of which we had many since we always had our cameras on hand to photograph our food. In one last notebook-like attempt, I put the pictures together into a several page memory book. On the last day of school we tried to stay focused on our duties in the front of the house, but it wasn't easy. In the side corners of the school's restaurant we signed each other's chef jackets and promised to stay in touch.

The day which we had been longing for had now arrived. We were done! It was really over.

Uncut - Chapter 46
Epilogue

"You wanted to know what it was really like, right?" I asked. The stranger nodded, seemingly at a loss for words. He glanced into the window and saw the students in the kitchen. The picture he was seeing clearly didn't match the story he had just heard. This, I understood very clearly. Nothing is ever the way you think it will be. One student told me a few weeks earlier that she was trying so hard to remember what it felt like to look into that window and want to attend the school more than anything in the world. I also remember that feeling.

In a hurry to start celebrating, I cut the conversation with the stranger short and wished him good luck in his cooking endeavors. After all this was the last day and I was ready to party! I was glad it was all over wasn't I? Wasn't it the biggest relief of my life to walk away from this school or was it actually anti-climatic for it to be over? I began to walk with my friend to our cars one last time

I heard the stranger yell "Hey" and I glanced over my shoulder, paused for a moment and stopped to look at him. As I stared back at him, I noticed in the background the huge, long windows of the brick front school. I glanced at my friend and said "Maybe it was fun?" She smiled and nodded her head, unable to speak through the haze of tears in her eyes.

I look back towards the stranger, who finished what he started to ask me. "Would you do it again Chef?"

THE END

Recipe List

Conversions

A pint is a pound, the world around!

3 Teaspoons = 1 Tablespoon
2 Tablespoons = 1 ounce
¼ cup = 2 oz.
½ cup = 4 oz.

1 cup = 8 oz. = 16 Tablespoons or 48 Teaspoons
2 cups = 1 pint = 16 oz, 32 Tablespoons, or 96 Teaspoons

2 pints = 32 oz. = 1 qt. = 4 cups, 64 Tablespoons, or 192 Teaspoons

4 quarts = 1 gallon 128 oz., 16 cups, 256 Tablespoons, or 768
     Teaspoons

To go from pounds to kilograms divide by 2.2.

1 lb. = 2.2 kilograms
1 oz. = 28.35 g.

To convert lbs. (oz). to grams multiply by 28.35
To convert pounds to kilograms multiply by 0.45
To convert grams to oz. divide by 28.35.
To convert fluid oz. to milliliters multiply by 30
To convert cups to liters multiply by 0.24
To convert quarts to liters multiply by 0.95
To convert gallons to liters multiply by 3.8

Knife Cuts

Fine Julienne 1/16" x 1/16" x 2"

Julienne 1/8" x 1/8" x 2"

Batonnet ¼" x ¼" x 3"

Brunoisette 1/16" x 1/16" x 1/16"

Brunoise 1/8" x 1/8" x 1/8"

Small Dice (Macedoine) ¼" x ¼" x ¼"

Medium Dice (Parmentier) ½" x ½" x ½"

Large Dice (Carre) ¾" x ¾" x ¾"

Tourne – 7 sided

Glossary of Cooking Terms

Absorption   Process in which one substance permeates another; a fluid permeates or is dissolved by a liquid or solid for example, <u>soaking up</u>.

Aciduler   To make a preparation slightly acidic, tart or tangy by adding a small amount of lemon juice or vinegar.

Aging   A process by which beef is held under controlled temperatures for a period of time.

A La Anglasie   Standard breading procedure.

Al Dente   Firm, but not soft or mushy to the bite. Refers to vegetables or pasta.

Allumette   Cut into matchstick shapes; usually refers to potatoes.

Aise   Means in the style of.

Aioli   Garlic mayonnaise

Almond Paste   Mixture of finely ground almonds and sugar

AP weight   As purchased; the weight of an item before trimming.

Aqua Culture   Farm raised fish.

Arborio Rice	A variety of short-grain rice from Italy.
Aromatic	Various plants, herbs and spices. For example bay leaf, parsley or ginger, that impart a lively fragrance and flavor to food and drink.
Argula	Type of green leaf. Means "rocket".
Au sec	Until dry.
Au Jus	Served with its natural juices. Usually unthickened pan drippings.
Bacteria	Microscopic organisms, some of which can cause disease, including food-borne disease.
Bacon	Pork that has been cured and smoked.
Bain-Marie	A hot water bath. A way of cooking or warming food by placing a container in a pot of very hot water. It used when food cannot be cooked over direct heat and for keeping delicate sauces hot.
Bake	To cook by dry heat. In meat, this is roasting.
Bake Blind	Technique for baking an unfilled pastry shell. The unbaked shell Is pierced evenly with a fork to keep it from puffing up.
Barbeque	To cook with dry heat created by the burning of hardwood or by the hot coals of this wood.
Baste	To moisten meat with a liquid while cooking, to add flavor and to prevent drying of the surface.
Batonnet	Cut into sticks about ¼" x ¼" x 2 ½"-3".
Batter	Semi liquid mixture containing flour or other starch used for the production of products such as cakes and breads and for coating products to be deep-fried.

BBQ Ribs	Ribs from all species prepared by barbecuing.
Béchamel	A sauce made by thickening milk with a roux.
Belly Burn	Flesh eaten away in an animal or fish due to adrenaline right before their death.
Beurre Manie	A mixture of equal parts raw butter and flour (raw roux) mixed together to form a paste. Emergency thickener.
Beurre Noisette	Brown butter. Butter that is cooked until a light brown.
Bi-valve	A mollusk with a pair of hinged shells, such as clams and oysters.
Blanch	To cook an item briefly and partially in boiling water or in hot fat. It is frequently used to loosen peels from vegetables, fruits and nuts. It can also be used to partially cook French fries or other food or to prepare for freezing.
Blanquette	A white stew made of white meat or poultry simmered without preliminary browning and served with a white sauce.
Bob Veal	Meat of very young beef and dairy animals. Usually less than 21 days old.
Boil	Cook in water or another liquid that is bubbling rapidly; 212°F. at sea level.
Bouquet Garni	Combination of fresh herbs tied together in a leek leaf or two celery sticks and used for flavoring stocks or soups.
Bourride	Stew of monkfish from Provence, France. Hot broth with the addition of cold mayonnaise.
Braise	To brown meat in a small amount of fat, then cook slowly in a covered utensil in a small amount of liquid.

Bread Flour	Strong flour used for breads.
Breaded	Product that is coated with less than 30% of an edible substance, usually flour or bread crumbs. Product may be first dipped in a batter to enhance the adherence of the breading.
Brioche	Popular French bread. Rich yeast dough containing large amounts Of eggs and butter.
Broil	To cook with radiant heat from above.
Broth	A flavorful liquid obtained from the simmering of meats and/or vegetables.
Brown Sugar	Regular granulated sucrose containing various impurities that give it a distinctive flavor.
BRT	Boned, Rolled, & Tied. A way to order lamb.
Brunoise	Vegetables cut into very small regular cubes.
Butter cream	An icing made of butter and/or shortening blended with Confectioner's sugar or sugar syrup and sometimes other Ingredients.
Cake Flour	A fine, white flour made from soft wheat.
Calf	Calf is differentiated from veal on the basis of lean color. Calf has a grayish red to moderately red lean color, while veal is usually grayish pink.
Capon	A castrated male chicken.
Caramelization	Browning of sugars caused by heat. Carmelization occurs at 338°F.
Carcass	The dressed, slaughtered animal, containing two sides.
Carry over Cooking	The rise in temperature in the inside of roast meat after it is removed from the oven.

Cartilage	A tough, elastic, fibrous connective tissue found in various parts of the body, such as the joints, outer ear, and larynx. A major constituent of the embryonic and young vertebrate skeleton, it is converted largely to bone with maturation.
Chef	The person in charge of a kitchen or of a department of a kitchen.
Ciseler	Means to mince.
Channel Fat	Fat located over the vertebrae on the inside surface of beef chucks, ribs and loins. Also on the inside surface of pork loins.
Chateaubriand	The center cut portion of the whole completely trimmed tenderloin; which has the same size diameter on both cut ends and is reasonably uniform in girth with a minimum of tapering. Cooked and served as one piece.
Chicory	Bitter green. Ex: Belgian Endive, Curly Endive, Radicchio Escarole.
Chinois	China cap sieve. A conical strainer.
Chiffonade	'Torn into rags' Leafy herbs and greens that are finely shredded. Ex: used to cut basil, sage.
China Cap	A cone shaped strainer.
Chop	Meat which has bone in.
Chowder	Hearty American soup made from fish, shellfish and or vegetables. It usually contains milk and potatoes.

Clarify	To clear a cloudy liquid by removing the sediment. Most common method is to add egg whites and or eggshells to a liquid, like a stock and simmer for 10-15 minutes . The egg whites attract particles in the liquid much like a magnet works. After cooled, the mixture is poured through a sieve to strain out all residue. To clarify butter is to purify butterfat by removing milk solids.
Clarified Butter	Purified butterfat with water and milk solids removed.
Clear meat	A mixture of ground meat, egg whites, and flavoring ingredients used to clarify consommés.
Coagulation	Proteins being heated and causing them to denature and become firm.
Collagen	Connective tissue in meats that dissolves when cooked with moisture.
Compote	A dish of fresh or dried fruit which as been cooked slowly in a sugar syrup. In some cases, the syrup may contain liquor or spices. Slow cooking is important in the fruit keeping its shape.
Compound butter	Butter with something added. (ex: sage butter). Soften unsalted butter, chop sage and mix in.
Concasse	Rough cut of tomatoes which have been peeled and skinned.
Condiments	A savory, piquant, spicy or salty accompaniment to food. Examples are a relish, sauce or a mixture of spices.
Confectioner's Sugar	Sucrose that is ground to a fine powder and mixed with a little cornstarch to prevent caking.
Connective Tissues	Cartilage and collagen.

Consommé   A rich, flavorful, seasoned stock or broth that has been clarified to make it perfectly clear and transparent.

Coulis   A sweetened fruit puree used as a sauce.

Court Bouillon   Poaching liquid for fish made from vinegar or wine and water.

Cream of Tartar   Tartaric acid is a fast acting fine white crystalline acid salt that is a byproduct of the wine making industry. Cream of tartar is a component of baking powder in many baked goods. It stabilizes egg whites during whipping and allows them to reach maximum volume.

Crepe   Very thin pancake.

Cross contamination   The transfer of bacteria to food from another food or from equipment or work surfaces.

Crouton   Day old French bread dipped in butter, sprinkled with pepper and baked until crisp. Used to top French Onion soup.

Crustaceans   Sea animals with segmented shells and jointed legs such as shrimp and lobsters.

Cuisson   Leftover liquid from poaching.

Cured   Meat products which have been infused with special saline solutions and ingredients to enhance flavor and color and extend shelf life.

Custard   Liquid thickened or set firm by the coagulation of egg protein.

Cutlet   Boneless meat.

Danish Pastry   A yeast risen, butter and egg enriched sweet pastry dough made using the same techniques as puff pastry and croissants.

Darne	Fish steak 1 ¾", bone in
Deckle	Fat cap on meat.
Deep Fry	To cook submerged in hot fat.
Deglaze	To swirl a liquid in a sauté pan to dissolve cooked particles which are scraped from the bottom of the pan.
Delmonico Steak	A boneless steak cut from the beef rib. Rib-eye steak.
Depouillage	Take a ladle to center of liquid in a pot to remove scum.
Demi-Glace	Meat, fish or chicken stock reduced to a concentrated form. Modern demi glace: reduced veal stock.
Demi-sac	Half dry.
Denature	Effect of heat on proteins.
Docking	To poke hole in pie crust before baking.
Dollop	A small scoop or mound usually referred to as whipped cream or a custard sauce used to garnish pastry or dessert.
Dorure	Egg wash used to add color to dough before it is baked.
Drawn Fish	Eviscerated, tail and head on.
Dressed Fish	Eviscerated, no scales, no gills.
Dry Aged	Fresh meat cuts which have been stored for various periods of time under controlled temperatures, humidity and air flow to avoid spoilage and ensure flavor, enhancement, tenderness and palatability. Prior to cutting or trimming, a dry aged product will have a firm, hard surface on exposed edible tissue.

Dutch Process Cocoa   Cocoa that has been processed with an alkali to Reduce its acidity.

Duchesse Potatoes   Potato puree mixed with butter and egg yolks. Piped from pastry bag.

Duxelle   A coarse paste or hash made of finely chopped mushrooms sautéed with shallots.

Edamane   Soy bean.

Egg wash   Egg wash is made from a whole egg, an egg yolk or an Egg white beaten together with milk, cream, or water. Egg wash is brushed on top of baked goods before they are baked to aid in even browning and to give them a shiny, crisp outer surface.

Emincer   To cut into very thin slices.

Emonder   To skin. To remove the skin from fruits and vegetables by heating.

Emulsion   Two opposing liquids brought together by agitation and the addition of an emulsifier.

Emincer   To cut into very thin slices.

Epepiner   To de-seed.

Ergot   Fungus on rye which resembles the rye itself.

Espagnole   A sauce made of brown stock and flavoring ingredients and thickened with a brown roux.

Evaporated Milk   Canned, homogenized milk that has had half of its water removed through evaporation.

Extract   A pure extract is made from concentrated natural oils, derived from plants that are mixed with alcohol.

Fabricated cuts   Cuts made from primal and sub-primal cuts. Fabricated cuts can be boneless or bone-in.

Fat Back   Fresh layer of fat that runs along the back of a pig. It is used to make crackling and lard for cooking. It is popular in Southern recipes.

Fat Bloom   White layer of fat released due to heat in improper storage (chocolate).

Fermentation   The process by which yeast changes carbohydrates into carbon dioxide gas and alcohol.

Filet Mignon   A steak cut from a beef tenderloin.

Fine Herbs   Italian Parsley, Chervil, Chives, Tarragon.

Flash Point   The lowest temperature at which the vapor of a combustible liquid can be made to ignite momentarily in air.

Flavorings   The effects of adding something to affect the taste and aroma of food. For example, a spice.

Fleur   One leaf; no stem attached.

File   Ground sassafras root.

Flounder   Flat fish from the Coast of California. Sweet fish

Foam   Process of beating eggs, with or without sugar to incorporate air. Foams made with whole eggs are used to leaven sponge cakes. Angel food cakes and meringues are leavened with egg white foams.

Fois Gras   Goose liver. Luxury item. Grade A is best.

Fold   Technique used to combine a light and heavy mixture and Retain the air that has been beaten into the lighter mixture.

Fond	Stock.
Fondue	Melted.
Fond Lié	A sauce made by thickening brown stock with cornstarch or another similar starch.
Fondant	A type of icing made of boiled sugar syrup that is agitated So that it crystallizes into a mass of extremely small white crystals.
Food Danger Zone	The temperature range of 41º F to 140ºF in which bacteria grow rapidly.
Fortify	To strengthen or enrich a food. Adding stock to chicken stock fortifies it. Also known as doubling.
Frangipane	Almond flavored cream.
Fricassee	A white stew in which the meat is cooked in fat without browning before liquid is added.
Frisee	A variety of curly endive or chicory that is more tender and lighter in color than curly endive.
Frittata	A flat open omelet.
Frizzle	To fry thinly sliced meat such as bacon over high heat until crisp and slightly curly in shape.
Fry	To cook in fat or oil. Applied especially to cooking in a small amount of fat, also called pan-frying; and to cook in a deep layer of fat, also called deep fat frying.
Fumet	A flavorful stock, usually made from fish.
Galette	Piece of dough.
Ganache	Rich cream made of equal parts whipping cream and chocolate.

Garnish	Decorative edible items used to enhance the eye appeal or add ornament to another food item.
Gelatin	Water soluble protein extracted from animal tissue, used as a jelling agent.
Gelatinazation	Process of heating starch in water which causes the starch to swell.
Gelee	Gelatin, aspic; meat or fish stock that has been clarified and then set with gelatin.
Glace	Sauce that has been reduced by removing moisture.
Glace de Viande	Meat glaze; a reduction of brown veal stock.
Glucose	Simple sugar available in the form of a clear, Colorless, tasteless syrup.
Gluten	Substance made up of protein present in wheat flour that gives structure and strength to baked items.
Gnocchi	Little pillows. Italian potato dumpling.
Goulash	A Hungarian stew flavored with paprika.
Grade	USDA designation that indicates quality or yield of meat.
Grains	Cereal includes any plant from the grass family that yields an edible grain or seed. The most popular grains are barley, millet, oats, rice, quinoa, corn, rye, wheat and wild rice.
Gratin	Dish topped with cheese or bread crumbs which are mixed with pieces of butter and then heated in the oven until brown and crispy.
Gratinee	To brown on top.
Gremolata	Italian parsley, lemon peel, garlic. All minced.

Gumbo	Can be made with any kind of meat. Traditionally made with Shrimp.
Hard Wheat	Wheat high in protein.
Haricot	Bean.
Herb	Fragrant leaves of any of many annual or perennial plants that grow in temperature climate and don't have woody stems.
Herbs de Provence	Dried herbs from southern France. Lavender, Rosemary, Thyme, Sage and Marjoram.
Hollandaise	Hot emulsion sauce made from egg yolks and clarified butter and flavored with lemon juice.
Holy Trinity	Cajun mirepoix. Celery, onions and green pepper.
Honey	A sweet, thick liquid made by honey bees. Used as a sweetener.
Ice Cream	A churn-frozen mixture of milk, cream, sugar, flavorings, and sometimes eggs.
Icing	A sweet covering and filling for cakes and Pastries, used in all types of desserts, pastries and confections. Made primarily of sugar.
Infusion/Infuse	Flavor extracted form an ingredient such as herbs, fruit or tea leaves by steeping them in a hot liquid. Sauces flavored with herbs are called infusions.
IQF	Individually Quick Frozen. Example: shrimp.
Italian Meringue	A meringue made by whipping a boiling sugar syrup into egg whites.
Jasmine rice	Aromatic rice.
Julienne	Cut into very fine strips.

Kabob	Boneless dices of meat which are generally placed on skewers and grilled. Also known as brochette meat and cube meat.
Kansas City Steak	Strip loin steak. Bone in or boneless. Also referred to as a New York Steak.
Knead	Technique for working dough until smooth and supple.
Lard	Pork fat that has been rendered.
Lardon	A small piece or strip of slab bacon.
Leading Sauce	A basic sauce used in the production of other sauces. The five leading hot sauces are Béchamel, Veloute, Espagnole, Tomato and Hollandaise. Mayonnaise and Vinaigrette are often considered leading cold sauces.
Legumes	A plant that has seed pod which are split along both sides when ripe. Beans, lentils, peanuts, soybeans and peas are some examples. Legumes are high in protein.
Lekvar	A Hungarian specialty. Thick spreadable preserve made of fruit with the skin left on and cooked with sugar. It is usually made from prunes or apricots.
Linzertorte	Tart made of raspberry jam and a shortbread dough with spices and nuts.
Liaison	Cream and egg yolks. It is a binding agent which is used to thicken sauces and soups. Ratio is 1 egg yolk to 1 cup of cream.
London Broil	Applies to a variety of beef cuts, usually boneless that can be broiled and then thinly sliced.
Macédoine	A mixture of vegetables or fruit cut into small cubes.
Macerate	To soak product (such as fruit) in liquid and Sugar to infuse the flavor.

Maitre d'Hotel butter	Compound butter containing parsley and lemon juice.
Marbling	Intramuscular fat; flecks of fat within the lean. Important factor affecting quality in meat. It enhances palatability by increasing juiciness and flavor.
Marinate	To be labeled marinated, a product must use a marinade that is a mixture in which food is either soaked, massaged, tumbled or injected in order to enhance taste, tenderness or other sensory attributes such as color or juiciness.
Marzipan	Paste or confection made of almonds and sugar and used for decorative work.
Marrow	An edible substance found in the center or bones.
Marrow Bones	Refers to the large round bones and shank bones of the round and chuck which contain significant amounts of marrow. The bones are usually cut into shorter pieces to expose the marrow.
Matignon	Edible mirepoix. Includes a pork product such as ham.
Medallion	Usually small, round slices of meat. Also known as Tournedos when cut from beef tenderloins.
Meuniere	The style of the millers wife (dusted in flour)
Milk Chocolate	Sweetened chocolate containing milk solids.
Mirepoix	Mixture of rough-cut or diced vegetables, herbs and spices. It is used for flavoring.
Mignonette	Means small.
Molasses	Heavy, brown syrup made from sugar cane.
Mollusk	A soft bodied sea animal, usually inside a pair of hinged shells such as clams or oysters.

Monter au Beurre   Finish with butter.

Monkfish   Non-bony fish. Poor man's lobster.

Mousseline Force   Meat   Chicken, Turkey, Salmon, Lobster.

Mutton   Yearling lamb. Most common.

Myotomes   Meat/flesh of fish.

Myocommata   Muscle between the meat of fish – makes fish flake.

Nappe   To cover. Consistency is like heavy cream. Means to coat your food.

Nappage   Thick jelly in different flavors. Used to cover Fruit as a finishing glaze in tarts.

Needling   A tenderizing process involving penetration of muscles by closely spaced thin blades with sharpened ends which cut muscle fibers into short segments.

New York   Bone in or boneless beef strip loins or steaks.

Neutral   A solution or compound that is neither acidic nor alkaline.

Offal   Another name for variety meats.

Olive Oil   Pressed from ripe olives, olive oil is highly prized. Used for desserts, pastries and confections as well as savory dishes and salads.

Overnight Fermentation   Slower fermentation. Usually in the refrigerator.

Ovine   Lamb.

Pancetta   Pork belly.

Pan broil	To cook uncovered in a frying pan. Fat is poured off as it accumulates.
Pan fry	To cook in a small amount of fat.
Papillote	Steam in paper.
Parfait	Type of sundae served in a tall, thin glass or frozen dessert made of egg yolks, syrup and heavy cream.
Pastry	Baked item made with a crusty of dough. Generally sweet, such as a pie or cream puff. Savory pastries such as Shepherd's pie may also be made.
Pastry Cream	Thick custard sauce which contains eggs and starch. It is made on The stove top.
Paupillete	To roll (fish).
Pectin	Soluble plant fiber used primarily as a jelling agent for fruit preserves or jams.
Pesto	Classic pesto contains basil leaves, pine nuts, parmesan cheese, garlic and olive oil.
Petit Four	A delicate cake or pastry small enough to be eaten in one or two bites.
Pilaf	Rice or other grain product that has been first cooked in fat and then simmered in a stock or other liquid, usually with onions, seasonings or other ingredients.
Poach	To cook gently in water that is hot, but not bubbling. Temperature is 160°-180°F. Shallow poach: liquid 2/3 up product. Start on stove, finish in oven. Sauce made from cuisson. Submerged poach: Stove top. Product completely submerged. Liquid not used for sauce.
Poele	To roast in butter.

Pot de Crème   A rich baked custard.

Potage   A soup that is in between a thin broth and a thick soup. It is usually pureed an dish often thickened with cream or egg yolks.

Poussin   A young chicken weighing a pound or less.

Porcini   "ini" means little pig.

Primal cuts   Basic major cuts into which carcasses and sides are separated.

Prime Rib   Rib roast.

Profiterole   Choux ball filled sweet or savory fillings. Best known is a dessert filled with vanilla ice cream and served with chocolate sauce.

Protein   Proteins are found in both animal and vegetables such as fish, meat and eggs. They are composed of amino acids and supply energy and building of body tissues.

PSMO   Peeled beef tender, side muscle on.

Puff Pastry   A very light, flaky pastry made from a rolled in dough and leavened by steam when baked.

Pumpernickel Flour   A coarse, flaky meal made from whole rye grains.

Punch   Method of expelling gases from fermented (bread) dough.

Puree   Food that has been mashed or strained to make a pulp that is smooth.

Purge   The juices exuded from fresh, cooked and cured meat cuts after the are packaged and which remain in the package at the time of opening.

Quail	A small game bird now domestically raised, usually weighing 6 oz or less.
Quenelle	Small oval portion of food formed with two spoons.
Quiche	Savory tart with a creamy egg base.
Raft	Coagulated clear meat that forms when stock is clarified.
Ragout	French word which means to stimulate the appetite. It is usually a thick, well-seasoned rich stew of meat, fish or poultry which is made with and/or without vegetables.
Ragu	Staple of northern Italy's Bologna, ragu is a meat sauce usually served with pasta. It usually contains tomatoes, ground beef, celery, carrots, onions, white wine and seasonings.
Ragouter	Means to stimulate the appetite.
Ratatouille	Dish made form red peppers, onions, tomatoes, zucchini, eggplant and often olives.
Rechauffer	French word for reheated or food warmed over. Literally means to rehash.
Réduire	To reduce; to heat a liquid on or to reduce it in volume by boiling.
Reduction	A liquid that has been concentrated by cooking it to evaporate part of the water.
Remouillage	Re-wetting." A stock made from bones that have already been used for stock; it is weaker than a first-quality stock and is often reduced to make glaze.
Rendering	Extracting fat from pork belly.

Riblette	A portion of pork or lamb back rib bones which may contain some fat and lean.
Riso	Rice.
Risotto	Italian dish of rice cooked in stock and butter.
Rhizome	Grows above and below the ground. Ex: ginger Cut against the grain.
Roast	To cook food by surrounding them with hot, dry air in an oven or on a spit over an open fire.
Roesti Potatoes	Boiled potatoes that have been grated and formed into small cakes and pan-fried until crisp.
Royal Icing	A form of icing made of confectioner's sugar and egg whites.
Royale	Custard.
Roulade	To make round.
Roux	Equal parts butter and flour. It is a cooked mixture.
Sachet	Mixture of herbs and spices tied in cheesecloth.
Salmonella	A widespread food-borne disease, spread by improper food handling and inadequate sanitation.
Salt Pork	Fat which is salt-cured. It is cut form the pig's belly and sides.
Sans	French for without.
Sausage	Common meat products prepared with meat or meat by-products and seasoned with spices in small amounts. Sausage products may be cooked or uncooked and smoked or unsmoked.

Sear	To brown surface of meat by brief application of intense heat.
Semolina	A hard, high-protein flour often used for the best quality macaroni products.
Sauté	Means "to jump". Cook at high heat, with low amount of fat. Dry cooking method.
Scone	A type of biscuit or biscuit like bread.
Seasonings	Ingredients added to food to intensify or improve the flavor. Most common seasonings are herbs such as rosemary, basil and oregano o and spices like cinnamon, cloves, and nutmeg. Vinegars are also popular seasonings and salt and pepper.
Sherbet	A frozen dessert made from water, sugar, fruit juice and sometimes milk or cream.
Shrink	Weight loss form meat/meat products which may occur throughout the product's life.
Simmer	Cook in water or other liquid that is bubbling. Temperature is approximately 185° to 200°F.
Simple Syrup	Combination of equal parts sugar and water. Flavor may be added.
Sirloin	Portion of the beef hindquarter remaining after the round, short loin and flank are removed. Steaks cut from this item are called sirloin steaks.
Simple Syrup	Equal parts sugar and water. The syrup is prepared by combining the water and sugar in a saucepan and brining to a boil to dissolve the sugar.
Singér	To sprinkle with flour at the start of cooking in order to eventually give a certain consistency to the sauce.
Slack roux	More fat than flour to allow for sweating of vegetables.

Slurry	Mixture of raw starch and a cold liquid which is used as a thickening agent.
Small Sauce	A sauce made by adding one or more ingredients to a leading sauce.
Smoke Roasting	To cook with dry heat in the presence of wood smoke.
Smoked	Meat cuts which have been exposed to the dry smoke of hardwoods, or which have had liquid smoke applied externally or as a cure ingredient.
Sous Chef	Second to the chef.
Smoke Point	When fats are heated they begin to break down. When fats become very hot they deteriorate quickly and begin to smoke. The temperature at which this deterioration happens is the smoke point.
Soft Wheat	Wheat low in protein.
Sourdough	A yeast type dough made with a sponge or starter that has fermented to the point of being sour. Used to make bread.
Spaetzle	Means little sparrow. Small dumplings or noodles made from a thin egg and flour batter.
Spices	Part of a plant other than the leaves which is used to flavor foods.
Sponge	A batter or dough of yeast, flour and water that is allowed to Ferment and is then mixed with more flour and other ingredients to make a bread dough.
Spun Sugar	Angel's hair. Used to decorate desserts. It is made from caramel.
Squab	Young, domestically raised pigeon.

Staling	The change in texture and aroma of baked goods due to the loss of moisture by the starch granules.
Steam	To cook by direct contact with steam.
Stew	To simmer a food or foods in a small amount of liquid that is usually served with the food as a sauce. A dish cooked by stewing, usually one in which the main ingredients are cut in small pieces.
Sub-Primal Cuts	Smaller cuts derived from primal cuts.
Supreme Sauce	A sauce made of chicken veloute and heavy cream.
Sweating	Cook a vegetable in fat until it is soft and translucent.
Sweetbreads	The thymus glands of calves used as food.
Tart	Flat baked item consisting of pastry and a sweet or Savory topping or filling similar to a pie, but usually thinner.
Tasso ham	Cajun cuisine. Boston butt or picnic shoulder cured with TCM, sugar, salt and rubbed with spices of cayenne, paprika, black pepper.
Tempering	Raising the temperature of a cold liquid by gradually introducing a hot liquid to it.
Thorax	Main body (head & lungs) of a lobster.
Texas Ribs	Beef back ribs.
Tomalley	Liver of a lobster.
Trocon	Piece of fish cut 2-3 darnes thick.
Tourne	A seven sided football like cut. Used for potatoes.

Tripe	The muscular stomach lining of beef or other meat animals.
Tri-Tip	Also known as the triangle. Beef.
Tranche	Cut at 45 degree angle.
Trussing	Tying the legs and wings against the body of poultry to make it a solid, compact unit.
Univalve	A mollusk with a single shell, such as abalone.
Vacuum Packed	Refers to the process of encasing meat cuts in bags or pouches fabricated from laminated plastic, evacuating air form the bags and sealing them for extended refrigerator storage.
Variety meats	Various organs, glands and other meats that don't form a part of the dressed carcass.
Velouté	A sauce made by thickening white stock with a roux.
Vino	Wine.
Wash	A liquid brushed onto the surface of a product usually before baking.
Whole Wheat Flour	Flour made by grinding the entire wheat kernel including the bran and germ.
Whole Fish	Scales on.
Yield Grade	These grades are designed to identify carcasses for differences in cutability or yield and are applied by the USDA Grading Service.
Zest	The colored part of the peel of citrus fruits.

About the Author

Patrice Johnson grew up in Bowie Md. She holds a Bachelor of Science degree in Business Management from the University of Maryland.

Prior to attending culinary school, she worked as a weapons contracts negotiator for the United States Navy for 12 years.

She enjoys fitness and has been an American Council on Exercise Certified Personal Trainer and Group Exercise Instructor since 1993.

Ms Johnson graduated with high honors from the California Culinary School of Arts in Pasadena, California, in 2002.

She resides in the small town of Ridgecrest, CA with her husband and two dogs and one cat. She has written a newspaper column entitled On the Menu for the Daily Independent Newspaper in her hometown.

She currently owns and operates her own personal chef business, Mystique.

Her hobbies when she is not cooking include wine tasting, traveling, camping and fantasy football and reading.

Ms. Johnson has always enjoyed cooking, but never imagined herself as a professional chef! As a young girl, she enjoyed baking with her mom and grandmother. The family had many special baking traditions which come from her Slovak heritage.

She is by her own admission NOT a pastry chef.

Made in the USA
Lexington, KY
31 May 2010